RACE AND REVOLUTION

D0176131

THE MERRILL JENSEN LECTURES
IN CONSTITUTIONAL STUDIES

Sponsored by

The Center for the Study of
the American Constitution

The State Historical Society
of Wisconsin

RACE AND REVOLUTION

Gary B. Nash

MADISON HOUSE

Madison 1990

Rancho Santiago College
Orange Campus Library

Nash, Gary B.
Race and Revolution

Copyright © 1990 by Madison House Publishers, Inc.
All rights reserved.

Printed in the United States of America.

No part of this book may be used or reproduced in any manner
without written permission from Madison House Publishers, Inc.,
except in the case of reprints in the context of reviews.

LIBRARY OF CONGRESS CATALOGING IN PUBLICATION DATA

Nash, Gary B.
    Race and revolution / Gary B. Nash. — 1st ed.
      p.   cm.
    Includes bibliographical references and index.
    ISBN 0-945612-11-7 (alk. paper)
      1. Slavery—United States—Anti-slavery movements.   2. United
    States—History—Revolution. 1775–1783—Afro-Americans.   3. United
    States—History—Revolution. 1775–1783—Social aspects.
    4. Abolitionists—United States—History—18th century.   5. Afro-
    Americans—History—To 1863.   6. United States—History—
    Confederation. 1783–1789.   I. Title.
E446.N37   1990
973'.0496073—dc20   90-36359
                                                                        CIP

ISBN 0-945612-11-7 (HC)
ISBN 0-945612-21-4 (PBK)

Printed on acid-free paper by Edwards Brothers, Inc.
Designed by William Kasdorf
Typeset and produced for Madison House
by Impressions, Inc., Madison, Wisconsin

Published by Madison House Publishers, Inc.
P.O. Box 3100, Madison, Wisconsin 53704

FIRST EDITION

E 446
N37 1990

CONTENTS

FOREWORD

As THE FOREMOST PROGRESSIVE HISTORIAN of the third quarter of the twentieth century, Merrill Jensen has had a profound impact on how we understand our past. Just as his writings influenced a generation of students, Merrill Jensen's interpretations of the Revolutionary era resonate today in the teaching and research of the almost fifty scholars who earned Ph.D.s under his direction. In this way, his ideas have been carried on by this next generation of neo-progressive historians.

While Professor Jensen confined his scholarship largely to political, institutional, and economic history, he was not unaware of or unconcerned about the importance of social, cultural and intellectual studies. For the most part however, he focused his writing and teaching on what he knew best—the political and economic conflicts in each of the thirteen states and their impact on the new nation. He understood that under the Articles of Confederation power originated with the states, and that is where his research always began.

Throughout his scholarship, Merrill Jensen emphasized the role of sectionalism in state and national politics. According to his interpretation, slavery was the most important issue in the politics that so divided the Revolutionary generation. He was well aware of how slavery and anti-slavery feeling repeatedly collided on the national political scene during the war years, in the various attempts to amend the Articles of Confederation, strengthen Congress, and to draft and ratify the new federal Constitution.

In this first series of The Merrill Jensen Lectures in Constitutional Studies, Gary B. Nash examines the Revolutionary fervor for liberty and the climate it created for the emancipation of slaves. For a brief moment in history, it seemed that the national division over slavery was susceptible to a peaceful and humane resolution. In his second essay, Nash demonstrates how, with independence and their effort to form a more perfect union, Americans tragically lost the zeal to free the thousands of African-Americans tyrannized by the institutions of slavery. Much of the blame for this failure to fully implement the promises of Revolution and liberty, according to Nash, must be laid on northern leaders. Nash, in his third essay, demonstrates how the free black community responded to their retrenched role in the new republic—and how they adjusted to an increasingly hostile white society, both north and south, that refused to accept them as equals. The Center for the Study of the American Constitution, established at the University of Wisconsin–Madison, is pleased to inaugurate The Merrill Jensen Lectures in Constitutional Studies with these lectures by Professor Nash.

Madison, February 1990   JOHN P. KAMINSKI

PREFACE

THE ESSAYS IN THIS BOOK grew out of The Merrill Jensen Lectures in Constitutional Studies, given at the University of Wisconsin in Madison in September 1988. I felt honored at the invitation to give the inaugural Jensen Lectures because he had always been for me a seminal thinker. Over the years I had also come to understand that part of his appeal to me was the steady course he maintained in his studies of Revolutionary America through the 1950s and 1960s when those who minimized conflict in American history were in their heyday. A son of the Progressive school, Jensen never doubted his instincts, and because he always returned to the sources he found plenty of evidence to replenish his convictions about the founding era—that this country gained its independence and laid down the foundations of government amidst an internal struggle between those who were democratically inclined and those who were aristocratically inclined. It was a view that lost popularity after World War II, and it was Jensen who by keeping an interpretive flame alive provided a crucial bridge between the Progressive school of the interwar period and the so-called "new social historians" of the last twenty years or so.

My introduction to Merrill Jensen came in 1952 when Wesley Frank Craven assigned *The New Nation* to his undergraduate class on the American Revolution at Princeton University. Frank Craven and Merrill Jensen became friends during World War II when they worked together in the U. S. Air Force history project. Craven's understanding of history was much less populist than Jensen's, and he gave much less weight to economic factors in history; but Craven admired Jensen's ability to challenge the received wisdom that argued the nearly complete failure of government under the Articles of Confederation (and hence justified the conservative reaction to revolutionary radicalism in the 1780s), and he had no doubt that no better book could be assigned to the young men at Princeton who were learning about the "critical period" of American history.

It was not until 1962 that, as a graduate student, I read Jensen's earlier book, *The Articles of Confederation*, published in 1940. After that, I tried to keep up with everything that Jensen published. More than anyone else, it seemed to me, he penetrated the heroic surface of events as he wrote about the revolutionary era. He brought to life the gritty realities of life and demonstrated the contingency of events in a Revolution that many historians had portrayed as a kind of American rendezvous with destiny. In a festschrift essay for his mentor, one of Jensen's students, E. James Ferguson, speaks of Jensen's "sympathy for the common man [combined] with a realistic sense of human motives and a hardheaded recognition of how loaves and fishes are divided." It is precisely these two characteristics of Jensen's work that drew me to him.

Jensen wrote virtually nothing about race or the institution of slavery. Nor, apparently, did he teach about race, at least to judge by the dissertation topics of nearly fifty doctoral students who took their training under him. The work of these students has enormously advanced our understanding of financial, economic, legal, and, above all, political history in the era of the

American Revolution. But race was not a historical problem that interested Jensen and therefore he ignored its importance in American history.

Perhaps a farm boy from South Dakota, who remained thoroughly midwestern all his life, had little reason to be attracted to the topic of race. But the logical extension of Jensen's lifelong and bowel-deep fascination with the democratic aspects of the American Revolution—with "the American Revolution within America," as he titled a series of essays he gave near the end of his career—*is* a concern with the question of slavery and race during the revolutionary era. The American Revolution involved multiple agendas, and some of the most important and fascinating of them were fashioned by black and white revolutionists who saw race as the great "American dilemma" long before a Swedish sociologist employed that term. These lectures are an exploration of this theme.

o   o   o

I am grateful to a number of people who have supported and criticized these essays. John P. Kaminski, editor of *The Documentary History of the Ratification of the Constitution*, a project that was brought to the University of Wisconsin and revitalized by Merrill Jensen, invited me to give the lectures. He and his fellow editors, Gaspare J. Saladino and Richard Leffler, offered important criticisms and generously provided citations for materials that had escaped my notice. John Murrin, at Princeton University, read portions of the manuscript and helped me rein in several interpretive wild horses I had unleashed. Michael Kay at Toledo University, Graham Hodges at Colgate University, and Michael Fitzgerald at St. Olaf College gave me an opportunity to try out some of my ideas on perceptive audiences at their campuses and offered important critiques of their own. At UCLA, Tom Ingersoll, David Finch, and Paula Scott provided invaluable research assistance.

RACE AND
REVOLUTION

An official symbol of abolitionist societies in both England and America sent a mixed signal: the text implies equality while the illustration shows the black as both pious and submissive. *The Library Company of Philadelphia.*

ONE

The Revolutionary Generation Embraces Abolitionism

AMONG THE MOST IMPORTANT ADVANCES in our understanding of the American Revolution in the last generation is the realization of the degree to which the revolutionaries were brought to recognize the incompatability between the slave-labor system in which most of the colonies were deeply involved, either as slaveowners or slavetraders, and the principles that underlay the struggle against England and the creation of a new nation. It is striking to browse among nineteenth- and early twentieth-century histories of the United States and find how thoroughly historians from Abiel Holmes and John Gorham Palfrey in the antebellum period to postbellum historians such as Hermann von Holst, George Bancroft, Henry Adams, John Fiske, and Woodrow Wilson ignored the antislavery impulse that grew during the revolutionary era. Not more than an occasional comment survives from these historians to indicate how significantly the question of slavery and race relations reverberated in the last third of the eighteenth century. It is one instance of what Leon Litwack noted in his presidential address to the Organization of American Historians in 1987—that American historians have consistently underestimated "the depth, the persistence, the pervasiveness, the centrality of race in American society" and in so doing have "perpetuated and reinforced an array of racial stereotypes and myths and easily justified the need to repress and quarantine black people."[1]

In considering the Revolutionary period, these earlier historians were bound by the chains of Whiggish history. Fixated on the creation by white colonists of a political system founded on republican principles, they found little about the benighted black fifth of American society in the 1770s and 1780s to spark their interest. Of course, in writing about the Constitutional Convention they could not entirely ignore the question of slavery, but by the time of the Convention the high tide of abolitionist sentiment was already receding.

Among early twentieth-century Progressive historians, as Staughton Lynd has shown, the question of race received even less attention. Max Farrand, whose documentary record of the founding fathers became standard reading for two generations, excused the nation's leaders for not abolishing slavery by arguing that the majority "regarded slavery as an accepted institution, as a part of the established order."[2] With these words, Farrand casually dismissed several decades of antislavery activity and the emergence among many southern as well as northern leaders of a strong distaste for the institution. The two titans of the Progressive school of history—Frederick Jackson Turner and Charles A. Beard—were similarly inattentive, saying so little about the revolutionary generation's struggle over the issue of slavery as almost to excuse the institution.[3]

In the 1950s and early 1960s, when the Consensus historians, who stressed the absence of conflict in American history, reached the height of their influence, historical judgments on abolitionism reached a new low. A number of historians found antebellum abolitionism a topic worth studying, but their assessment of the antislavery advocates would hardly have encouraged a new consideration of the revolutionary generation's

4

encounter with slavery. Readers of American history learned that the abolitionists of the antebellum era, who had long been charged by historians as impractical, immoderate, and often unsavory firebrands, were almost clinically obsessed.[4] By extension, the revolutionary crisis of conscience over slavery became a fleeting aberration, a chimera. A corollary of this attitude toward abolitionism was an indifference to the question of slavery itself; for, as Lynd points out, "tolerance towards the institution of slavery and intolerance toward the abolitionist movement are attitudes usually found together, for they support and supplement each other."[5]

Even as the Civil Rights movement of the 1960s and 1970s created an intense interest in the seventeenth- and eighteenth-century roots of America's race problem, many historians continued to deny that the founding fathers could have done anything about slavery, even though they recognized it as an evil and understood that it contradicted the ideological assumptions of the revolutionary cause. In 1971, Donald Robinson, in a large book entitled *Slavery in the Structure of American Politics*, argued that "no leading politician was brooding much about Negro slavery, or seriously at work on plans to loosen its hold on the nation's life" between 1765 and 1780.[6] In the same year, Bernard Bailyn, who only four years before had written at length on the revolutionary generation's attempts to grapple for the first time with the massive contradiction that slavery posed for a republican government based on principles of natural rights, partially reversed himself by contending that, while the colonists recognized that slavery was brutal and degrading, they regarded life in general for most laboring free people as such.[7] "Only gradually," wrote Bailyn, "were men coming to see that this was a *peculiarly* degrading and a *uniquely* brutalizing institution." Thus, he concluded, the revolutionaries ought to be congratulated for not pushing harder for abolition, which would have been to allow "the revolutionary movement to slide off into fanaticism."[8] By employing the word "fanaticism," Bailyn returned to the vocabulary of proslavery apologists of the antebellum period, who entrenched that word, as Larry Tise has recently written, "in the proslavery glossary of overworked epithets."[9]

In offering a political explanation for the failure of the revolutionary generation to abolish slavery, historians of our era have usually cited the fragility of the new nation and the certainty of its leaders that an attempt to force abolition on the southern states would shatter the political union that had held together so shakily during and after the war. Some recent explanations even returned to the view advanced by John Ticknor Curtis in 1903 in his *Constitutional History of the United States*. While implying that slavery in the Chesapeake might have been abolished, Curtis opined that if the deep South had not been accommodated on the question of slavery, Georgia and the Carolinas would have refused to join the union, and the failure to achieve union would have brought about "a war of races, or . . . a frightful oppression of the slaves."[10]

This essay and the one that follows reject such views and offer a different explanation of why the transformation in sentiment about slavery after the Revolution led only to compromises that left the institution intact and in fact provided it the protection of the vastly strengthened federal government after 1788, leaving for future generations the business that could not be done by the revolutionaries themselves. In particular, I wish to stress the role of the northern states in the failure to abolish slavery and to show how economic and cultural factors intertwined in what was not a judicious decision by the leaders of the new American nation but their most tragic failure.

Five interlocking factors in the 1770s and 1780s made this the opportune time for abolishing slavery. First, it was the era when the sentiment for ridding American society of the peculiar institution was the strongest. Second, it was the moment when the most resistant part of the new nation, the lower South, was most precariously situated and thus manifestly ill-prepared to break away from the rest of the states. Third, it was a period when the system of thought called environmentalism was in full sway, suggesting that the degraded condition of slaves was a matter of social conditioning, not innate inferiority. Fourth, it was a time when the opening of the vast trans-Appalachian West provided the wherewithal for a compensated emancipation. Lastly, it was the era when the use of this western domain as an instrument for binding the nation together had moved to the forefront of the public mind and when the existence of this vast unsettled territory as part of a national domain provided an area where the free slaves could be colonized if they were not to be permitted to remain in the settled parts of the country.

o   o   o

Only in recent years have historians demonstrated how widely slavery was recognized as incompatible with the natural rights philosophy of the revolution. Bernard Bailyn himself did much to illuminate this. In *The Ideological Origins of the American Revolution* (1967) he concluded that the contradiction between slavery and revolutionary ideology "became generally recognized" and cited a Virginia pamphlet of 1765 to demonstrate the point for that largest of slaveholding colonies.[11] Bailyn had changed his view by 1973, when he wrote that members of the Continental Congress, meeting in Philadelphia, had only a "dawning awareness" of the evil of slavery and came only "gradually" to this recognition.[12] His earlier judgment is more nearly correct. Educated colonists had been much affected by Montesquieu's attack on slavery in *Spirit of the Laws*, published in 1748, and by Adam Smith's frontal condemnation of slavery in his *Theory of Moral Sentiments*, published in 1764. It was a reading of Montesquieu's work, and perhaps Smith's as well, that brought James Otis to include in one of the earliest defenses of colonial rights, *Rights of the British Colonies* (1764), the uncompromising assertion that "The Colonists are by the law of nature free born, as indeed all men are, white or black. ... Does it follow that tis right to enslave a man because he is black? Will short curl'd hair like wool, instead of christian hair, as tis called by those whose hearts are as hard as the nether millstone, help the argument? Can any logical inference in favour of slavery be drawn from a flat nose, a long or a short face?"[13]

Otis's pamphlet, based on a natural rights argument, was read throughout the colonies. It was soon complemented by a swelling chorus of clerical attacks on slavery that built upon the Quaker argument that slavery was sinful and that, as John Woolman argued, it corrupted white colonists who had debased Africans in America, turning them into a despised and degraded people. From this combined stream of thought, one religious, the other secular, the volume of antislavery protest grew rapidly in the late colonial period, as David Brion Davis has shown in splendid detail.[14]

But how deeply in the social structure and how widely across regions did the antislavery arguments based on natural rights and religious morality spread? Donald Robinson argues that the plight of the slaves "did not command much attention."[15] Much evidence to the contrary can be found, although obviously we can never determine precisely what the state of colonial opinion was on the subject. What is beyond dispute since the monumental work of Winthrop Jordan and David Brion Davis is that a voluminous literature on slavery in America and the problem it presented to the ideological foundations of the American case against Britain came off the printing presses and was available to the public in the 1760s and 1770s. Fathoming how this literature was received, however, has proved a much more daunting task.

Some means exist, however, to measure antislavery sentiment in different parts of American society. We know, for example, that in 1767, three years after Otis's *Rights of the British*

Colonists was published, the Massachusetts General Court debated a bill "to prevent the unwarrantable & unusual Practice ... of inslaving Mankind in the Province."[16] Though the bill failed, the debate portrays the rise of considerable sentiment that slavery was incompatible with the doctrine of natural rights. Bailyn tells us that three years later Samuel Cooke, in preaching the election sermon of 1770 "devoted most of his text to 'the cause of our African slaves.' "[17] In 1773, the issue of abolition was of sufficient general interest to be the subject of the Harvard College commencement debate.

Farther south in 1773, in the mid-Atlantic region, Benjamin Rush informed Granville Sharp, the English abolitionist, that the "spirit of liberty and religion with regard to the poor Negroes spreads rapidly thro'out this country." In May of the next year he wrote again that the "cause of African freedom in America" was still gaining ground; and in November 1774, shortly after the Continental Congress had completed its first meetings in Philadelphia, where Rush had an opportunity to become acquainted with many of the delegates, he described how the abolitionist spirit "prevails in our counsels and among all ranks in every province." Bailyn confirmed this observation when he concluded, after studying the prerevolutionary pamphlet literature, that the cry against slavery as incompatible with republican principles and cries of British oppression "had become a commonplace in the pamphlet literature of the northern and middle colonies."[18] Slavery, Rush predicted, in what would turn out to be a great miscalculation, would be totally moribund in America in forty years.

Part of Rush's optimism may have stemmed from the fact that the Continental Congress had debated the question of slavery and the slave trade and, in the second article of the Continental Association in 1774, pledged not only to forswear further traffic in slaves but to hire no vessels and sell no produce or manufactures "to those who are concerned in it." The slave-trade prohibition was not initiated by northern delegates but rather was inspired by the resolutions of a Virginia convention in early August that had banned the slave trade in that colony under charges, as the representatives from Fairfax County asserted, that they wished "to see an entire stop forever put to such a wicked, cruel, and unnatural trade."[19]

Was Rush totally naive in arguing that antislavery feeling permeated "all ranks in every province"? His knowledge of this is likely to have come from the discussions going on in the Pennsylvania Statehouse, where the Continental Congress met. Probably he exaggerated in the heightened—almost millennial—fervor of this time, but perhaps not so much as those historians who have maintained that the advance of antislavery opinion was slow and sporadic. In New England, the Calvinist clergy, who reached the broad mass of people, argued that for Americans to continue holding slaves was to deprive themselves of divine protection, for God would hardly tolerate the hypocrisy of those who enslaved others while fighting to secure their own liberty. "For shame," wrote Nathaniel Niles, "let us either cease to enslave our fellow-men, or else let us cease to complain of those that would enslave us."[20] Slaveholding, pronounced Samuel Hopkins, was a "sin of a crimson dye, which is most particularly pointed out by the public calamities which have come upon us, from which we have no reason to expect deliverance till we put away the evil of our doings. . . ." Hopkins believed that "God is so ordering it in his Providence, that it seems absolutely necessary something should speedily be done with respect to the slaves among us. . . ."[21] As Winthrop Jordan has argued, by the eve of the Revolution, there was in New England a "generalized sense of slavery as a communal sin."[22]

Jordan's evidence is based not only on sermons of New England's clergy lambasting slaveholding but on the renunciations that issued from town meetings, such as in Danbury and Norwich, Connecticut, and from the preamble of a law by the Rhode Island assembly in 1774 banning slave importations, where legislators made the more secular argument that the slave trade (and, by implication, slavery itself) contradicted the natural rights ideology.[23] Such sentiment was growing rapidly in the middle colonies as well, especially in Pennsylvania. Not only the Quakers had inveighed against slavery there; slavekeeping was also condemned as "wickedness" that would incur divine wrath by the influential Presbyterian Francis Allison as early as 1768. By 1773, Benjamin Rush had published a pamphlet calling slavery a "national crime" that would bring "national punishment;" two years later the newly arrived Thomas Paine was expostulating in print against slavery.[24]

Of course, antislavery sentiment could be expected to resonate most effectually in the North where only a tenth as many slaves toiled as in the South. If slavery were to be abolished, it was indispensable that Virginia and Maryland, where half of the blacks in the United States lived in 1776, take a leading role. It was the Chesapeake, moreover, that produced the white leadership that played a pivotal role in national affairs in the revolutionary era, leading the revolt against England, furnishing much of the leadership for the Continental army, and playing critically important roles in the shaping of the new government, both under the Continental Congress and at the Constitutional Convention.

In fact, the Chesapeake leadership was much infected by natural rights ideology and saw clearly the necessity of abolishing slavery. George Wythe, Edmund Pendleton, and Thomas Jefferson, charged with reformulating Virginia's laws in 1776, wrote a bill that emancipated all slaves born after the passage of the act, provided for their education at public expense, and proposed their removal to a new land when they reached adulthood.[25] In 1783, Jefferson was still of a mind to banish slavery from Virginia. In his draft of "A Fundamental Constitution for the Commonwealth of Virginia" he would have outlawed the introduction of any more slaves into the state and banished slavery "beyond the generation which shall be living of the 31st day of December 1800; all persons born after that day being hereby declared free." Years later, Jefferson wrote that "the public mind would not yet bear the proposition [of abolition]," and so the authors "thought better that this should be kept back, and attempted only by way of amendment."[26]

No one doubts that Jefferson and his colleagues were correct that the emancipation bill would have raised a storm of opposition among many if not most of the owners of more than 200,000 slaves. No fundamental change occurs in history without the opposition of those who see their interests adversely affected. But equally to the point is that there was much support in the Chesapeake for abolishing slavery by one means or another, not only among leaders such as Luther Martin and Gustavus Scott of Maryland, Caesar Rodney of Delaware, George Mason, Patrick Henry, Edmund Pendleton, George Wythe, Jefferson, and St. George Tucker of Virginia, but among the generality of people. The Marquis de Chastellux, the perceptive French general who toured Virginia in the spring of 1782, reported that Virginians in general "grieved at having slaves, and are constantly talking about abolishing slavery and of seeking other means of exploiting their lands." Chastellux apparently talked with many people about this and judged that "this opinion . . . is almost universally accepted," though inspired by different motives. Among the educated and among the younger generation of planters, he found that concern for "justice and the rights of humanity" lay at the root of antislavery sentiment; among the older generation, the concern was utilitarian, based on the expense and trouble of slave labor and the growing conviction that day laborers and white servants would serve better. Whatever the motives, Chastellux found great disgust "with that tyranny which they exercise over those who may at least be described as of their own species. . . ."[27] Such disgust was strong enough to produce a ban on further slave importation in Virginia's state constitution of 1776, and many believed that choking off further slave imports would bring about the gradual death of slavery itself.

The antislavery sentiment of the war years continued beyond the first blush of revolutionary idealism. In Philadelphia, delegates to the Continental Congress from all parts of the country witnessed the debate over abolishing slavery in that state that occurred from 1778 to 1780 in the same building where Congress met. Attuned to the preamble of the Pennsylvania constitution passed in 1776, that avowed "that all men are born equally free and independent, and that they have certain natural, inherited, and inalienable rights," a determined group pressed for legislative action beginning in 1778. Calling slavery "the opprobrium of America," they proposed a gradual emancipation that would regain Americans the respect of "all Europe, who are astonished to see a people eager for Liberty holding Negroes in Bondage."[28]

Placed before the public in newspapers for the constitutionally mandated purpose of airing the issue, the bill's language could not have failed to reach members of the Congress. Its preamble gave a little lesson in history, calling attention to the tragic retrogression of human progress in the New World where "the practice of domestic slavery, so highly detrimental to morality, industry, and the arts, has been, in the instance of the natives of Africa and their descendants, in modern ages revived among Christians." Thus, America had been "made the scene of this new Invasion of the rights of mankind after the spirit of Christianity had abolished it from the greater part of Europe."[29] Of special significance in the drafting and passage of the bill was that Pennsylvania's Quakers were not involved since their wartime pacifism had stripped them of political power. Instead, it was Presbyterians, led by the tenacious George Bryan, who were principally responsible for the bill's passage, though Quakers worked behind the scenes.

By 1783, tenderness on the subject of slavery was so general in Congress that John Jay, negotiating in Paris on the terms of the peace, proposed that British subjects be forbidden to carry slaves to the United States, "It being the Intention of the said States," Jay argued, "intirely to prohibit the Importation thereof."[30] Another indication of the widespread sensitivity about slavery can be found in the debate over counting three-fifths of the slaves for the purpose of apportioning taxes among the thirteen states. The delegates, according to William Paterson of New Jersey, were "ashamed to use the term 'Slaves' & had substituted a description."[31] All "white and other free citizens and inhabitants" would be counted in determining the proportion of taxes to be paid by each state, but only "three fifths of all other persons not comprehended in the foregoing description" would be counted.[32] By 1785, Jefferson was so sanguine about the spread of antislavery feeling north of the Chesapeake that he thought the opponents of the cause no more numerous than the occasional robbers and murderers who roamed the countryside and predicted that "in a few years there will be no slaves Northward of Maryland."[33]

The momentum for rooting slavery out of the republican soil of the new nation was further advanced in the 1770s and 1780s by the rise of evangelical Christianity in the South. For men like Freeborn Garretson and David Rice slaveholding was one of a set of interlocking sins that included gambling, horse-racing, and sabbath-breaking—all afflictions of the self-indulgent gentry class. "Religious rebirth," as David Brion Davis puts it, "required, along with other renunciations, the voluntary manumission of slaves."[34] Among the Methodists—the fastest growing denomination in the Chesapeake and by the mid-1780s a considerable force in Virginia, Maryland, and Delaware—the antislavery gospel was spread by leaders such as Francis Asbury and Thomas Coke, who circulated resolutions condemning it in the early 1780s. In the famous Christmas meeting of 1784, the Methodist leaders banned from joining Methodist society all those who held slaves and called upon all slaveholders to provide for the manumission of their chattel property at specified times, as Quakers had already done. We view, they wrote, "the Practice of holding our Fellow Creatures in Slavery . . . as contrary to the Golden law of God on which hang all the Law and the Prophets, and the unalienable Rights of Mankind, as well as every Principle of the Revolution." The next spring, led by Asbury and Coke, the Methodists solicited the support of Washington and petitioned the House of Delegates in Virginia to enact a gradual general emancipation of slaves.[35] Although the bill was dismissed, it was not, according to James Madison, "without an avowed patronage of its principle by sundry respectable members."[36]

Many southern Methodists dug in their heels on the issue of slavery and forced the church to yield on its strong anti-slavery stance. Yet like Devereaux Jarrett, a Methodist minister in Virginia who owned 24 slaves, they did not doubt that slavery must be abolished. The abolitionist views of Asbury and Coke angered Jarrett; yet he wrote in 1790 that he was "well pleased that a spirit of liberation is prevailing" and predicted that slavery would wither away.[37]

Like Jarrett, a great many of Virginia's leaders, trusting in what Martin Duberman has called "the benevolent workings of time," were convinced that slavery would soon die after slave importations ceased.[38] Jefferson wrote a French correspondent in 1786 that there were "men enough of virtue and talent in the General Assembly to sponsor" an abolition act, "but they saw that the moment for doing it with success was not yet arrived."[39] In the following year, residents of several counties petitioned the Virginia legislature to eradicate slavery, employing the natural rights earlier evoked so frequently in the North. "The Glorious and ever memorable Revolution can be Justified," wrote the inhabitants of Frederick and Hampshire counties, "on no other Principles but what doth plead with greater Force for the emancipation of our Slaves in proportion as the oppression exercised over them exceeds the oppression formerly exercised by Great Britain over these States."[40]

Such petitions in 1787 came just after Jefferson had written Richard Price, the English radical, in phrases that echoed Benjamin Rush's belief that antislavery sentiment was spreading rapidly. Jefferson's letter was prompted by Price's pamphlet on the importance of the American Revolution, where the Englishman had included slavery on his list of dangers to the future of the republic and had declared that until it was abolished "it will not appear that they [the Americans] deserve the liberty for which they have been contending."[41] Heartily endorsing Price's pamphlet, Jefferson, then serving as U. S. minister to France, wrote that "from the mouth to the head of the Chesapeak, the bulk of the people will approve of it [the extirpation of slavery] in theory, and it will find a respectable minority ready to adopt it in practice, a minority which for weight and worth of character preponderates against the greater number, who have not the courage to divest their families of a property which however keeps their consciences unquiet." Jefferson believed that the abolitionist feeling was stronger in Virginia than in Maryland because in the former state young men "under preparation for public life" had "sucked in the principles of liberty as it were with their mother's milk."[42] Most of the milk was being dispensed at the College of William and Mary by George Wythe, Jefferson's mentor in the law and the man whom Jefferson, as wartime governor, installed at the College as professor of law. Jefferson described Wythe as "one of the most virtuous of characters" and a man "whose sentiments on the subject of slavery are unequivocal."[43]

Jefferson's own *Notes on the State of Virginia*, completed in 1786, provide further evidence of the strength of antislavery sentiment. To be sure, this much controverted book contains passages revealing Jefferson's deep-seated belief in the innate inferiority of blacks. But it also contains the central question of the time in matters of race—whether "the liberties of a nation [can] be thought secure when we have removed their only firm basis, a conviction in the minds of the people that these liberties are of the gift of God? That they are not to be violated but with his wrath?" Jefferson went on with his famous passage condemning slavery for "the unremitting despotism" it required of the master. Focusing on slaveowners rather than slaves, he averred that few could escape the depravity involved in the exercise of "the most boisterous passions" necessary to subdue unwilling slaves. But following this passage is the less quoted statement that reveals how Jefferson himself felt as a statesman wrestling with the snare of slavery. "And with what execration should the statesman be loaded, who permitting one half the citizens thus to trample on the rights of the other, transforms those into despots, and these into enemies, destroys the morals of the one part, and the amor patriae of the other." Jefferson could already see a perceptible change "since the origin of the present revolution. The spirit of the master is abating, that of the slave rising from the dust, his condition mollifying, the way I hope preparing, under the auspices of heaven, for a total emancipation, and that this is disposed, in the order of events, to be with the consent of the masters, rather than by their extirpation." Appended to the *Notes* was a draft of a law that declared free "all persons" born after December 31, 1800.[44]

Further signs that the newly independent Americans recognized slavery as a grave national problem (and one that could not be dismissed except by imperiling the republican system of values that celebrated free labor and abhorred slavery as a relic of an archaic past) can be found in the liberalization of laws in the South regarding manumission and also in the large number of manumissions. In 1782, Virginia repealed the prohibition on private manumissions passed in 1723. Delaware and Maryland passed similar acts in 1787 and 1790, and by the latter year "manumission was a slaveholder's prerogative throughout the South, except in North Carolina."[45] Though the decreasing viability of slave labor in areas of the upper South that for a generation had been making the transition from tobacco to wheat farming had much to do with individual decisions to manumit slaves, there was in every manumitter, we might suppose, strong sentiment that slavery was immoral and unnatural. Otherwise owners of slaves who could no longer be profitably employed would merely have sold their bondsmen and bondswomen to planters in areas where slavery was still profitable.

In a few cases, such as the manumitting of aged slaves with no capacity to work, altruism could be entirely absent; but the manumitting documents themselves include language infused with the revolutionary doctrine of natural rights, often interwoven with statements of Christian conscience. "The constant reiteration of antislavery ideals," writes Ira Berlin, "suggests that most manumitters took them to heart." When one man freed slaves because, to quote one Virginian, "it is contrary to the command of Christ to keep fellow creatures in bondage," his neighbors were often affected.[46]

The rapid growth of the free black population in the upper South thus gives a final, if rough, indication of antislavery sentiment. Maryland's free black population, which was 1,817 in 1755, reached 8,000 by 1790 and nearly 20,000 by the turn of the century. In Virginia, where a census in 1782 revealed 1,800 free blacks, the number swelled to nearly 13,000 in 1800 and 20,000 a decade later. Delaware's free black population, only 3,899 in 1790, swelled to 8,268 in 1800 and 13,136 in 1810. Even with these increases, free blacks made up only one-twelfth of the upper South's blacks by 1800 and two percent of those in the lower South.[47] But such figures should not be dismissed as unimportant, for they indicate that even in the absence of a compensated gradual emancipation law, thousands of slaveholders were disentangling themselves from the business of coerced labor. Such was not often the case in South Carolina and Georgia to be sure, but throughout most of the country, in the upper South as well as the North, the feeling had spread widely that slavery was incompatible with the principles of the Revolution, that it could not be reconciled with Christian morality, and that it was an unsatisfactory basis for the economy of the new nation.

In sum, by the mid-1780s, those of abolitionist persuasion in the United States could take considerable satisfaction with the progress that had been made and could think themselves anything but fanatical in pushing forward to cleanse their society of slavery. During the war slave importations had entirely ceased, and most states were forbidding its reopening. In Massachusetts the Superior Court held in 1783 that slavery was incompatible with the state's constitution, particularly with its bill of rights, which asserted that "all men are born free and equal." New Hampshire similarly abolished slavery by judicial decree. Vermont had outlawed slavery, and Connecticut, Rhode Island, and Pennsylvania had all passed gradual abolition laws. Debates over abolition were occurring in New York and New Jersey. In the Confederation Congress in 1784 only the absence of a New Jersey delegate, confined to his chambers with illness, prevented the achievement of the seven state votes necessary to ban slavery from the western territories. As it was, Jefferson from Virginia and one of North Carolina's delegates voted for the ban.[48] In the upper South the combined weight of Quakers, Methodists, and natural rights proponents had made abolishing slavery an issue commanding serious debate in the legislatures, and in 1788 Maryland's Attorney General, Luther Martin, declared that slavery was "inconsistent with the *genius* of *republicanism* and has a tendency to *destroy* those *principles* on which it is *supported*, as it *lessens* the *sense* of the *equal rights* of *mankind*, and habituates us to *tyranny* and *oppression*."[49]

David Cooper of New Jersey may not have been far off the mark in declaring that in America "we need not now turn over the libraries of Europe for authorities to prove that blacks are born equally free with whites; it is declared and recorded as the sense of America."[50] Cooper was a Quaker and a dedicated abolitionist, so his judgment might be doubted. But Benjamin Rush in 1787 was equally sure of "the prevalence of sentiments favorable to African liberty in every part of the United States," though doubtless Rush mistook opinion in Georgia and the Carolinas.[51] George Washington in 1786 told Lafayette that he believed gradual abolition "certainly might, and assuredly ought to be, effected."[52] None of these many leaders of the revolutionary generation found the idea of abolition fanatical. In fact a great many of them regarded it as unthinkable that a republic based on natural rights theory could survive without the emancipation of the enslaved fifth of the population. Indeed, a "general consensus," as David Brion Davis has written, emerged in the three decades after 1760 "that black slavery was a historical anomaly that could survive for a time only in the plantation societies where it had become the dominant mode of production."[53] A moment of epic importance, a transformative moment, seemed at hand.

NOTES

1. Leon Litwack, "Trouble in Mind: The Bicentennial and the Afro-American Experience," *Journal of American History*, 74 (1987), 317, 326.
2. Max Farrand, *The Fathers of the Constitution: A Chronicle of the Establishment of the Union* (New Haven, 1921), 130, quoted in Staughton Lynd, *Class Conflict, Slavery, and the United States Constitution* (Indianapolis, Ind., 1967), 180.
3. Lynd, "On Turner, Beard, and Slavery," in Lynd, *Class Conflict*, 135–52.
4. Fawn M. Brodie, "Who Defends the Abolitionists?" and Martin B. Duberman, "The Northern Response to Slavery" in Martin B. Duberman, ed., *The Antislavery Vanguard: New Essays on the Abolitionists* (Princeton, N. J., 1965), 52–67, 395–413.
5. Lynd, "On Turner, Beard, and Slavery," 143.
6. Donald L. Robinson, *Slavery in the Structure of American Politics, 1765–1820* (New York, 1971), 55.

7. Bernard Bailyn, "The Central Themes of the American Revolution: An Interpretation," in Stephen G. Kurtz and James H. Hutson, *Essays on the American Revolution* (Chapel Hill, N. C., 1973), 29; Bailyn's earlier position on the problem of slavery is set forth in his *The Ideological Origins of the American Revolution* (Cambridge, Mass., 1967), 232–46.

8. Bailyn, "Central Themes," 29.

9. Larry E. Tise, *Proslavery: A History of the Defense of Slavery in America, 1701–1840* (Athens, Ga., 1987), 29.

10. John Ticknor Curtis, *Constitutional History of the United States From the Declaration of Independence to the Close of their Civil War* (New York, 1903), 516–17.

11. Bailyn, *Ideological Origins*, 235–36.

12. Bailyn, "Central Themes," 29.

13. James Otis, *Rights of the British Colonies Asserted and Proved* (Boston, 1764), 29.

14. David Brion Davis, *The Problem of Slavery in Western Culture* (Ithaca, N. Y., 1966), Part III.

15. Robinson, *Slavery in the Structure of American Politics*, 85.

16. Louis S. Gerteis, *Morality and Utility in American Antislavery Reform* (Chapel Hill, N. C., 1987), 8.

17. Bailyn, *Ideological Origins*, 239.

18. Ibid.; Benjamin Rush to Granville Sharp, October 20, 1773; May 13, 1774; Nov. 1, 1774, in John A. Woods, ed., "The Correspondence of Benjamin Rush and Granville Sharp, 1773–1809," *Journal of American Studies*, 1 (1967), 3, 5, 13.

19. Quoted in Robinson, *Slavery in the Structure of American Politics*, 79.

20. Quoted in David Brion Davis, *The Problem of Slavery in the Age of Revolution, 1770–1823* (Ithaca, N. Y., 1975), 292.

21. Quoted in ibid., 294–95.

22. Winthrop D. Jordan, *White Over Black: American Attitudes Toward the Negro, 1550–1812* (Chapel Hill, N. C., 1968), 297–98.

23. Ibid., 291.

24. Francis Alison to Ezra Stiles, Oct. 20, 1768, quoted in Jordan, *White Over Black*, 299; [Benjamin Rush], *An Address to the Inhabitants of the British Settlements in North America, upon Slave-Keeping* ... (Philadelphia, 1773), 30.

25. For the 1776 bill on abolishing slavery, see Julian P. Boyd et al., eds., *The Papers of Thomas Jefferson* (Princeton, N. J., 1950–), II, 672–73. For the draft of the 1783 constitution, see ibid., VI, 298.

26. Thomas Jefferson, "Autobiography," in Paul Leicester Ford, ed., *The Works of Thomas Jefferson* (12 vols.; New York, 1904–5), I, 76–77.

27. Howard C. Rice, Jr., trans. and ed., *Travels in North America in the Years 1780, 1781, and 1782 by the Marquis de Chastellux* (2 vols.; Chapel Hill, N. C., 1963), II, 439.

28. *Pennsylvania Packet*, Nov. 28, 1778; Arthur Zilversmit, *The First Emancipation: The Abolition of Slavery in the North* (Chicago, 1967), ch. 5 for a general account of the Pennsylvania law. (See Documents, pp. 112–14.)

29. *Pennsylvania Packet*, March 4, 1779.

30. Richard B. Morris, ed., *John Jay: The Winning of the Peace, Unpublished Papers, 1780–1784* (New York, 1980), 540.

31. Max Farrand, ed., *Records of the Federal Convention of 1787* (3 vols.; New Haven, Conn., 1911), I, 561.

32. Merrill Jensen, John P. Kaminski, and Gaspare J. Saladino, eds., *Constitutional Documents and Records, 1776–1787* (Vol. I of *The Documentary History of the Ratification of the Constitution*, Madison, Wis., 1976–), 148–50.

33. Thomas Jefferson to Richard Price, Aug. 7, 1785, Boyd, *Papers of Thomas Jefferson*, VIII, 356.

34. David Brion Davis, *Slavery and Human Progress* (New York, 1987), 136.

35. Albert Matthews, "Notes on the Proposed Abolition of Slavery in Virginia in 1785," Colonial Society of Massachusetts *Publications*, 6 (1904), 370–80.

36. James Madison to George Washington, Nov. 11, 1785, William T. Hutchinson et al., eds., *The Papers of James Madison* (Chicago and Charlottesville, Va., 1962–), VIII, 403.

37. Quoted in Tise, *Proslavery*, 37.

38. Duberman, *Antislavery Vanguard*, 402.

39. Thomas Jefferson to Jean Nicolas Demeuneir, June 26, 1786, Boyd, *Papers of Thomas Jefferson*, X, 62–64.

40. "Anti-Slavery Petitions Presented to the Virginia Legislature by Citizens of Various Counties," *Journal of Negro History*, 12 (1927), 671–73.

41. Richard Price, *Observations on the Importance of the American Revolution and the Means of Making it a Benefit to the World* (London, 1784, reprinted Boston, 1784), 15.

42. Thomas Jefferson to Richard Price, Aug. 7, 1785, Boyd, *Papers of Thomas Jefferson*, VIII, 357.

43. Ibid.; on Wythe's opposition to slavery, see also Robert M. Cover, *Justice Accused: Antislavery and the Judicial Process* (New Haven, Conn., 1975), 50–55.

44. Thomas Jefferson, *Notes on the State of Virginia*, ed. Merrill D. Peterson, *Thomas Jefferson: Writings* (New York, 1984), 288–89.

45. Ira Berlin, *Slaves Without Masters: The Free Negro in the Antebellum South* (New York, 1974), 29.

46. Ibid., 30.

47. The data is from the published federal censuses.

48. Boyd, *Papers of Thomas Jefferson*, VI, 611n; VII, 121n.

49. John P. Kaminski and Gaspare J. Saladino, eds., *Commentaries on the Constitution* (Vol. XV of *The Documentary History of the Ratification of the Constitution*, Madison, Wis., 1984), 433. (See Appendix.)

50. David Cooper, *A Serious Address to the Rulers of America, on the Inconsistency of Their Conduct Respecting Slavery* ... (Trenton, 1783), 12–13. (See Documents, pp. 124–25.)

51. Lyman H. Butterfield, ed., *The Letters of Benjamin Rush* (2 vols.; Princeton, N. J., 1951), I, 441–44.

52. Worthington C. Ford, ed., *The Writings of George Washington* (14 vols.; New York, 1889–93), XII, 240; the French visitor Brissot de Warville still found Washington favoring gradual abolition in 1788 but convinced by this time that most Virginians were not ready for it. Mara Soceanu Vamos and Durand Echeverria, trans. and eds., *New Travels in the United States, 1788* by J. P. Brissot de Warville (Cambridge, Mass., 1964), 238.

53. Davis, *Slavery and Human Progress*, 82.

The Philadelphian Edward Clay was the premier cartoonist of the Jacksonian era. His caricatures, such as "Johnny Q. introducing the Haitian Ambassador to the ladies of Lynn, Massachusetts," lampooned what he saw as the social pretensions of free blacks, and took dead aim at white abolitionists. (Detail) *The Library Company of Philadelphia.*

TWO

The Failure of Abolitionism

IF THE REVOLUTIONARY GENERATION drank deeply from the wells of antislavery ideology—if, as Winthrop Jordan has said, the question asked everywhere was not whether slavery should be abolished but when and how—why were such compromises made to slavery at the Constitutional Convention in 1787 and again in the last decade of the eighteenth century? And have historians properly cast the lower South as the principal villain in forcing the so-called "Compromise of 1787" by which slavery received protection from the new national government "at very little cost to the region" and the slave trade was protected for 20 years?[1] Moreover, have historians accurately singled out the fragile political union of northern and southern states as the key stumbling block to the abolition of slavery?

In explaining the failure of the new nation to come to grips with slavery, historians repeatedly have pointed to the precariousness of the newly forged union of the states and the intransigence of the lower South, particularly Georgia and South Carolina, in thwarting the widespread desire of those in the North and upper South to see the traffic in slaves ended forever and the institution of slavery set on the road to extinction. Two problems emerge here—one concerning political fragility, the other the strength of South Carolina and Georgia.

In regards to the argument of the precariousness of the revolutionary confederation of states, historians have never really considered that a national plan for abolishing slavery might have been an integrating rather than a divisive mechanism, helping to create a genuinely national society out of regional societies by eliminating a rankling sore in the body politic and completing a reform without which postrevolutionary American society could never be ideologically true to itself. No doubt the confederation of states was imperfectly knit together; but how was union to be strengthened? For the most part, historians have answered that question by becoming apologists for the revolutionary leaders who succumbed to the threats of the lower South. Thus, they have assumed that slavery could *not* have been abolished and have justified what did *not* happen. Their explanations reek of inevitability, almost always in historical writing an argument put forward by those whose mistakes are being excused and virtually never by those victimized by the mistakes. Hamilton wrote in *The Federalist* #85 that "a *nation*, without a *national government* is ... an awful spectacle";[2] but there were many who believed that a nation based on an abandonment of principles widely subscribed to during its blood-filled birth was also an awful spectacle. It is likely that a national referendum would have supported the proposition of Luther Martin of Maryland, enunciated in 1788, that "*slavery* is *inconsistent* with the *genius* of *republicanism*, and has a tendency to *destroy* those *principles* on which it is *supported*, as it *lessens the sense* of the *equal rights* of *mankind*, and *habituates* us to *tyranny* and *oppression*." Martin subscribed to the antislavery position argued at the Constitutional Convention, as he informed Marylanders during the ratification debates. "It was said," he reported, "it ought to be considered that *national* crimes can *only be*, and *frequently are*, *punished* in this world by *national punishments*, and that the *continuance* of the slave trade, and thus giving it a *national sanction* and *encouragement*, ought to be considered as *justly exposing* us to the *displeasure* and *vengeance* of *Him*, who is equal Lord of all, and who views with equal eye, the poor *African slave* and his *American master!*"[3]

Such poignant comments, often coming from the South as well as the North, tell us that in the eyes of many leaders the continuing presence of slavery left the union of states highly fragile from the day the Constitution took effect. It was a thought that tormented its chief architect, James Madison, until his death.[4]

The second objection to the political fragility thesis concerns the belligerent opposition of South Carolina and Georgia to all attempts to deal with the problem of slavery. Historians have been especially wont to point to the alleged ultimatum thrown down by South Carolina's delegate Thomas Lynch just 26 days after the Declaration of Independence—if it was to be debated "whether their Slaves are their Property, there is an end of the Confederation"—and by John Rutledge at the Constitutional Convention thirteen years later, when Rutledge exploded during the debate over imposing a tax on imported slaves that the "true question at present is whether the Southn. States shall or shall not be parties to the Union."[5] Historians have accurately interpreted the militant defense of the slave trade and slavery by South Carolina and Georgia. But perhaps they have not adequately considered whether these two states of the lower South were in a position to dictate national policy on the issue.

In fact, Georgia, and less so South Carolina, were precariously situated in 1787 and had far greater need of a strong federal government than the rest of the states had need of them. With the powerful Creek confederacy and the Spanish in Florida hemming them in and threatening them militarily, no states were more in need of the military power of a federal government in the late 1780s. In 1786 Creek war parties, under the leadership of Alexander McGillivray, had driven Georgian frontiersmen out of disputed areas in the Creeks' ancient homelands and had thrown the state "entirely on the defensive." South Carolinians and Georgians were quaking at the prospect of a backcountry pan-Indian alliance as the Convention got underway because McGillivray had just entertained a delegation of headmen from northern tribes. Georgia had even convened a special session of the legislature to deal with the emergency.[6]

It was this need of attachment to a strong national government that led George Washington to remark: "If a weak State, with powerful tribes of Indians in its rear & the Spaniards on its flank, do not incline to embrace a strong *general* Government there must, I should think, be either wickedness, or insanity in their conduct."[7] No doubt there was plenty of wickedness in Georgia but insanity there was not. Georgia's ratification convention rushed pell-mell to endorse the Constitution without a dissenting vote and almost without debate. They did so, said the state's first representative to Congress in 1789, "in full confidence that a good, complete, and efficient government would succor and relieve them [from the Creeks]."[8] This almost desperate condition makes Georgia's and South Carolina's threats to withdraw from the new nation if the new government addressed the issue of the slave trade and slavery ring somewhat hollow.

Granting the intense commitment to slavery among Carolinians and Georgians, what might have happened if South Carolina and Georgia had not been accommodated by the other states on the slavery issue and had refused to ratify the Constitution? Would they have established a separate status, and if so, how? Separate confederacies—northern, middle, and southern—were often proposed, the latest immediately before the Constitutional Convention met, but none of these received serious consideration. Would the states of the lower South have left the union to become part of Catholic Spain's American empire? Or would the states of the lower South have embraced the country against which they had fought in order to become a part of a British West Indian confederacy? If so, would the rest of the states have been deeply damaged at the loss of a paltry five percent of the nation's population? Georgia had caused general disgust during the war by contributing nothing at all to the fiscal quotas set by Congress, and the rumor in 1780 of peace terms that included the abandonment of Georgia and South Carolina to Great Britain brought no cries of distress from the northern delegates to Congress.[9] Most southerners admitted privately that even the entire South could hardly make it on its own. Monroe's report to Patrick Henry from the Confederation Congress the year before the Convention met, at a time when free navigation on the Mississippi created a North-South crisis, is revealing. If the confederation fell apart, Monroe ruminated, it was essential that Pennsylvania join the South.[10] Tench Coxe, one of the leading political economists of the period, made the same point in 1790, showing how thoroughly the economic fortunes of the Chesapeake region, and even North Carolina, were commercially linked to the North.[11]

As it turned out, South Carolina and Georgia did not have to contemplate what to do if the other states took a forceful position on the slave trade and slavery. To the delight of those in the lower South, northerners and Chesapeake leaders who had argued the necessity of banishing slavery because a republican society could not be built upon a foundation of coerced labor were willing to accept that they must live with the contradiction of slavery and republicanism. It was a willingness that had its source, as we will see, in northern unwillingness to participate in solving the problem of slavery.

Historians have been curiously reluctant to question whether South Carolina and Georgia were really in a position to hector the other states into believing they would abandon the union if abolition of the slave trade or a general emancipation were contemplated. They have been even more reluctant to consider how much responsibility the northern states bore in the exhaustion of the abolitionist movement after it reached its height in the mid- to late-1780s. This studied inattention to the North's role has been implicitly justified by the fact that the northern states swore to ban any further importation of slaves (as did most of the southern states) and, it is said, by the fact that they gradually freed those held in bondage within their own boundaries (although several northern states did not actually abolish the institution entirely until the 1840s). This left the South as the home of the system of compelled labor. In effect, northern gradual-abolition laws have gotten the North off the hook, persuading historians who were educated and who taught in the North for more than a century that slavery was a southern problem rather than a national problem. The regional animosity associated with the Civil War also suffused the consciousness of northern historians, heightening their tendency to ignore the fact that slavery was not simply a southern problem in the postrevolutionary era.

Pro-northern historians have been self-congratulatory and narrow of vision in this line of argument. In their own part of the country the gradual abolition laws were of great importance; but in fact most slaves got their release from bondage only by dying or running away, and their children were promised freedom only after long periods of indentured servitude.[12] But more important, slavery was a problem that a society in the process of self-definition after the Revolution could not avoid in *any* region, and most of those who spoke about national destiny recognized this. As a national problem, slavery required a national solution in which the North might have been expected to take the lead. There could be no truly national community, no durable union of southern and northern and western states, while slavery continued to grow within a republican system of government. As Madison would say some years later, in authoring his own emancipation scheme, "it is the nation which is to reap the benefit [of emancipation]. The nation, therefore, ought to bear the burden."[13]

Even in the ways that inhabitants of the northern states freed themselves from the stain of slavery they sent signals southward that weakened the antislavery impulse there in the late eighteenth century. Examples abound of prominent critics of slavery in the North who had difficulty freeing their own slaves. And in the manner northern state governments dealt with the abolition of slavery the South witnessed the central difficulty besetting the revolutionary generation—how to put into practice those beliefs that could be implemented only at personal cost. It was a problem that plagued North as well as South in the fledgling nation: in spite of much talk of Americans as a specially virtuous people, the revolutionary generation fell short of virtue when it came to what Jefferson called "the interesting spectacle of justice in conflict with avarice and oppression."[14]

Two individual cases in Philadelphia, played out in the 1780s for all members of the Continental Congress to see, illustrate the point. The Reverend Francis Allison, minister of the First Presbyterian Church and a denominational leader in the mid-Atlantic colonies, was convinced by 1768, even before antislavery pamphlets were coming from the press, that "the Common father of all men will severely plead a Controversy against these Colonies for Enslaving Negros and keeping their children[,] born British subjects, in perpetual slavery."[15] At the time he wrote this Allison owned four slaves, but he freed none of them until his death in 1779 and even then could not wholly give up his interest in them. On his death bed he added a codicil to his will, extending their service for several more years.[16]

An even more striking inability to sacrifice a pecuniary interest in slavery in order to be ideologically consistent was the behavior of Benjamin Rush. In 1773, while trying to build his medical practice in the Quaker capital, Rush had penned one of the strongest attacks on slavery read in the colonies to that date. Indicting slavery, Rush predicted that "national crimes require national punishment" imposed from on high unless "God shall cease to be just or merciful."[17] In the same year Rush wrote the English abolitionist Granville Sharp that he was heartened that whereas Anthony Benezet had "stood alone a few years ago in opposing Negro slavery in Philadelphia, now three-fourths of the province as well as the city cry out against it."[18] Yet about three years later Rush purchased a slave, William Grubber.[19] In 1783, while still holding Grubber in slavery, Rush wrote that "the advocates for the poor Africans" were "at present . . . considered as the benefactors of mankind and the man who dares to say a word in favor of reducing our black brethren to slavery is listned [sic] to with horror, and his company avoided by every body."[20] Rush could hardly have been unaware of the hypocrisy of his purchase of a slave. Yet even after joining the Pennsylvania Abolition Society in 1784, just after it was revived, the philanthropic doctor would not release Grubber.

But then, in 1787, Rush had a remarkable and disturbing dream occasioned by his reading of Thomas Clarkson's recently published *Essay on the Slavery and Commerce of the Human Species*, which in turn had been inspired by Anthony Benezet's *Historical Account of Guinea*, a reading of which had convinced Clarkson to devote his life to abolitionism. Rush recounted how after reading Clarkson's essay the figure of the saintly Benezet pursued him in his sleep. Transported nocturnally to a distant shore, Rush found himself standing on a sandy beach in a country of surpassing beauty. Approaching a grove of trees, he came upon a group of Africans gathered for religious observances. The natives fell into panic at the sight of the white man because, as one of them, a venerable old man, told him, the color white, "which is the emblem of innocence in every creature of God," was to Africans "a sign of guilt in man." The old African informed Rush that he was standing in the paradise that God had given to Africans who had been wrenched from their homelands and made to serve a life of ghastly brutality under slavery. One African after another came forward to relate tales of horrors experienced under slavery. Then, all eyes turned down the beach where an ancient, crippled white man was seen approaching. Coming closer, his face appeared "grave, placid, and full of benignity." In one hand he carried a petition and in the other a pamphlet on the unlawfulness of the slave trade. Then as he drew closer, the throng of blacks rushed to meet the "venerable figure" and began applauding. "And," recounted Rush, "I awoke from my dream by the noise of a general acclamation of—ANTHONY BENEZET!"[21]

This guilt-drenched dream converted Rush to the cause of abolitionism, and he soon began aiding free blacks with a passion. He threw himself into the work of the Pennsylvania Abolition Society, helping to write its constitution when it was reorganized a second time and incorporated in 1787 and serving as secretary. In the same year he wrote Jeremy Belknap, Congregational minister of Boston's Federal Street Church and friend of free blacks in that city, "I love even the name of Africa, and never see a Negro slave or freeman without emotions which I seldom feel in the same degree towards my unfortunate fellow creatures of a fairer complexion. . . . Let us continue to love and serve them, for they are our brethren not only by creation but by redemption."[22] In a few more years he would emerge as a bulwark of support for Philadelphia's free blacks when they launched a campaign to erect the first independent black church in the North. But Rush would hold Grubber a slave for seven years more. A New Englander found words that described perfectly the difficulties of men like Allison and Rush: slavery was "one of those evils that it will be very difficult to correct—Of all Reformations those are the most difficult to ripen where the Roots grow as it were in the pockets of men."[23]

Paralleling cases of how individual northerners dealt with slavery is the example of how state legislatures dealt with the problem. At this higher level is another example of how the revolutionary generation in the North drank very cautiously from the wells of republicanism, while keeping close track of their economic interests. Pennsylvania as the southernmost northern state, as the center of Enlightenment humanitarianism in North America, as the state whose capital provided the seat of national government, and as the site of the first American abolition society, is a particularly telling case. Pennsylvania's abolition law of 1780 has gained extensive notice as the first passed in America and has drawn effusive praise as exemplifying the spirit of enlightened reform in the Revolutionary era. The first historian of the Pennsylvania Abolition Society, writing in 1848, called it a law "which for justice, humanity, and philanthropy, has seldom been equalled, and which raises the State of Pennsylvania to a high position amongst the nations of the earth."[24] But in fact the Pennsylvania law was the most restrictive of the five gradual abolition laws enacted by the northern states from 1780 to 1804.[25] The law freed not a single slave; and in the process of debating the law, its original provision to free the children born of slave women at age 18 if they were female and age 21 if they were male was changed so that all children born after the law became effective were consigned to servitude until age 28. Thus it was possible for a female child born of a slave on the last day of February in 1780 to live out her life in slavery and, if she gave birth to children up to her fortieth year, to bring into the world in 1820 children who would not be free until 1848.

By this extension of the years of servitude the costs of gradual emancipation were transferred from slaveowners to the children of slaves. Given the life expectancy of laboring people— one commentator believed that most people "used to hard labour without doors begin to fail soon after thirty"—this provision offered Pennsylvania slaveowners what Fogel and Engerman have called "the opportunity to engage in philanthropy at bargain prices."[26] One disappointed reformer said as much at the time. David Cooper tore the mask of benevolence from the legislators: "If we keep our present slaves in bondage, and only enact laws that their posterity shall be free, we save that part of our tyranny and gain of oppression, which to us the present generation, is of the most value." Would America ever fulfill its promise, queried Cooper, if slaveholders told their slaves, "we will not do justice unto you, but our posterity shall do justice unto your posterity"?[27]

From the examples of northern persons and polities wrestling with the competing claims of conscience and material interests we can see that by the mid-1780s, when talk of a general emancipation was much in the air and when significant gains had been made on a number of fronts in cleansing the new republic of its deepest stain, the northern states had reached the point where their antislavery rhetoric could maintain motive force—the power to dictate outcomes—only if it led to concrete plans for the gradual abolition of slavery nationwide. How might the northern states have contributed to a national solution to the problem of slavery?

o   o   o

Two main problems confronted those who thought about ending slavery in America. The first was economic: how would slaveowners be compensated? The second was social: how would freed slaves be fit into the social fabric of the new nation? Solutions to these two thorny problems hinged, in turn, first on a willingness to make economic sacrifices; and second, on an ability to envision a truly biracial republican society. Northerners as well as southerners, as we will see, lost the abolitionist fire in their bellies on both of these cardinal points. They would never rekindle that fire in their own generation; and by the time they were in their graves the best opportunity for abolishing slavery had been lost. These two crucial points require detailed exploration.

The Economic Question

Nobody who thought about abolishing slavery imagined that those who held property in human beings could be deprived of it without compensation, for that would have amounted to an enormous confiscation of private property by a revolutionary generation that had seen property and human rights as closely intertwined. The view developed by post-1830 abolitionists, that no man should be rewarded for ceasing to commit a sin, had little currency at the time.

Could the new nation, saddled as it was with an enormous war debt, have financed such a compensated emancipation? In fact, such an idea was in the air. Gouverneur Morris, representing Pennsylvania at the Constitutional Convention, specifically stated his preference for "a tax for paying for all the Negroes in the U. States" rather than to "saddle posterity" with a Constitution that legitimated slavery.[28] Such a compensated emancipation would have had advantages for thousands of slaveowners in the upper South who were looking for opportunities to make the transition to a free-labor force. Reckoning 600,000 slaves at an average value of $150 in the postwar period, the cost would have been 90 million dollars. Such a sum, levied as a tax on the entire polity, would have amounted to something like $180 per family—a heavy sum for those days.

But the government had an alternate source of funds in the western lands, which were understood at the time to be enormously valuable. The sale of federal lands, spurred by a powerful tide of westward migration, writes Peter Onuf, "promised virtually inexhaustible revenues to promote the common interests of all the states and strengthen the national government."[29] Throughout the 1780s nationalists reminded Americans of the potential of the western lands. Pamphlets such as Pelatiah Webster's *Essay on the Extent and Value of our Western Unlocated Lands* (1781) spread the knowledge, as he exclaimed, that they were greater in extent than France, Spain, Germany, and Italy combined, containing more than half a billion acres of "the richest wild lands in the world."[30] Americans supposed in the 1780s that their population would continue to double every 25 years, sending hundreds of thousands of seaboard inhabitants spilling across the Appalachian Mountains into the river valleys of the Ohio and the Tennessee and beyond. Land was to be sold there at a minimum of $1 per acre; in fact, 1.3 million acres had been sold prior to the opening of the Land Office in 1800, and another 19.1 million acres were sold between that year and 1820. If the price per acre had been raised to $2, the millions of acres sold from 1785 on could have gone a long way toward underwriting a gradual compensated emancipation.[31]

The use of western lands in solving a national problem, and in helping to create a national and republican identity, was by no means beyond the imaginations of postrevolutionary Americans. In fact, the question of how the western lands would be regulated and made to work in the interest of national integration became a major issue of the mid-1780s. The entire debate over establishing orderly settlement and republican government in the western domain revolved around the notion that "a harmony of interlocking interests" between North and South must be achieved.[32] In fact, the Congress prohibited the carrying of slaves into the Northwest Territory, and southerners supported this prohibition. Yet at the time when North and South learned how to reconcile their differences over the western lands in the interest of an enduring national union, they implicitly agreed not to broach the problem of slavery in the states, even though many realized that while slavery remained, genuine union over an extended period would be almost impossible to maintain. In this decision the North was far more involved than has generally been recognized. No northerner came forward with a plan for a general or gradual emancipation worked out under the auspices of the national government, although northern leaders continued to point out that the cancer of slavery had to be removed before a healthy republic could be constructed. Thus Americans north of the Chesapeake demonstrated through their *in*action in the late 1780s that economic interest outweighed moral commitment when it came to participating in a national solution to the problem of slavery.

Shortly after the formation of a stronger federal government northern leaders reached the moment of truth. During the second session of the first Congress, meeting in New York early in 1790, the northern states had the opportunity to take action on the slavery issue when several groups of mid-Atlantic Quakers and the Pennsylvania Abolition Society petitioned Congress on February 11 and 12, imploring the nation's new legislative body to assert its powers, as implied in the preamble of the Constitution, to extend the blessings of liberty "without distinction of color, to all descriptions of people." The petition of the Society of Friends pointed out the "licentious wickedness of the African trade for slaves, and the inhuman tyranny and blood guiltiness inseparable from it." The Quakers asked for a "remedy against the gross national iniquity of trafficking in the persons of fellow-men." The more strongly worded petition of the Pennsylvania Abolition Society asked for Congress to use its power to destroy the slave trade and ameliorate slavery.[33] As it happened, the petitions arrived shortly after Congress had taken up Secretary of the Treasury Alexander Hamilton's Report on Public Credit, which proposed that the federal government assume and fund the revolutionary war debts of the states. At the beginning of that epic debate, which has absorbed historians looking at national politics in this year, the House of Representatives suddenly had to consider the matter of slavery, and, as it turned out, to stage a full-scale debate on the institution and the power of the national legislature to ameliorate it. The resulting press coverage—three newspapers covered the debate in detail, and their reports were reprinted in many other newspapers—brought the issue squarely before the public.[34]

Even the notion of dignifying the petitions by creating a special committee to consider them set off an acrimonious day-long debate on February 12, 1790. South Carolina's representatives tried to scuttle any debate by using the familiar argument heard at the Constitutional Convention that even to suggest that Congress had the power to tamper with slavery would tear the country apart. Representative James Jackson of Georgia spoke menacingly about how the petitions, if taken seriously, would "blow the trumpet of civil war."[35] However, many southerners joined northerners in the vote of 43 to 11 to establish the committee. In fact, the Maryland and Virginia representatives took the lead in supporting the motion to send the petitions to committee. At this point, it seemed clear that a large majority of the House had not been persuaded that Congress had no power at least to encourage a less oppressive system of slavery and especially to regulate the worst abuses of the slave trade; in fact, comments were frequently heard during the day's debate, as they had not been heard at the Constitutional Convention less than three years before, regarding the total abolition of slavery.[36] On the other hand, many northerners regarded the petitions as a major inconvenience. Tench Coxe, former secretary of the Pennsylvania Abolition Society but now assistant secretary of the treasury, recounted how he and others had made strenuous efforts to keep such petititons from being presented in 1789 and had eased off on trying to block similar attempts in 1790 "because it was believed that the public Debt would have been adjusted before it [the antislavery petititons] could be presented."[37]

It took more than two weeks, from the time it was appointed on February 15 with Abiel Foster of New Hampshire as chair, for the committee to hammer out its report on the antislavery petitions. During this time it listened to the arguments of a delegation of Quakers, mostly from Philadelphia, who pressed a number of antislavery pamphlets on committee members. This was one of the earliest examples of taking testimony from private parties and the first on the subject of slavery. The position of the Quakers and the Pennsylvania Abolition Society was straightforward: that "slavery is . . . an atrocious debasement of human nature" and that the preamble of the Constitution invested Congress with the power to "promote the welfare and secure the blessings of liberty to the people of the United States and, correlatively, that these blessings "ought rightfully to be administered without distinction of colour, to all descriptions of people. . . ."[38] The crucial element in the committee's deliberations concerned the power of Congress to regulate domestic slavery; those who supported the Quaker view that the preamble of the Constitution conferred such a power were defeated only after the chairman broke a tie vote.[39]

The Foster committee laid its report before the House on March 5, 1790.[40] While it goes too far to say that "the general spirit of the report was antislavery," as the main student of the debate has claimed, it is true that the report, at least as Carolinian and Georgian representatives read it, implied that after 1808 Congress might be free to regulate slavery as well as the slave trade.[41] William Loughton Smith of South Carolina exploded during the subsequent debates that "the memorial from the Pennsylvania society, applied in express terms for an emancipation of slaves, and the report of the committee appeared to hold out the idea that Congress might exercise the power of emancipation after the year 1808; for it said that Congress could not emancipate slaves prior to that period."[42] "Every clause of [the report]," claimed Aedanus Burke of South Carolina, "was drawn in ambiguous words and expressions, so as to involve in it, in some measure, such an interpretation as the Quakers wished for."[43] Certainly, deep southerners were alarmed at the entire matter. The Quakers' petitions "on the subject of slavery," wrote one Charleston resident, "has made as great an uproar . . . amongst the slave-holders, as St. Paul's preaching did among the silver-smiths at Ephesus. . . . I believe it would be more safe for a man to proclaim through this city that there was no God, than that slave-holding was inconsistent with his holy law"[44]

But during the debate on the Foster report, which began on March 16, northern support began to slip away. John Pemberton, the antislavery Quaker leader from Philadelphia, sat in the galleries and watched with disgust as the Georgia and South Carolina representatives harangued and filibustered against the report—verbal barrages that moderate Virginians such as Madison described as "shamefully indecent" and "intemperate beyond all example and even decorum."[45] Pemberton's disgust turned into dismay when New England and mid-Atlantic congressmen began to abandon their antislavery commitment, a few even abandoning the House altogether.[46] While deep southerners filibustered, delivering half-day speeches defending the slave trade as an act of humanity for rescuing blacks from African savagery and condemning Quakers as religious fanatics, no northerner rose to press the antislavery cause and only a few defended the slight openings that the Foster report had devised to ameliorate the conditions of the slave trade and slavery. Pemberton immediately saw the connection between their collapsing principles concerning slavery and their intense desire to adopt Hamilton's funding program, which would implement their vision for the economic development of the country. "The funding system is so much their darling," wrote Pemberton, "that they want to obtain the favor of those from Carolina and Georgia."[47]

So completely did the northern representatives bow down to the lower South that only the negative votes of the Virginia delegation kept the South Carolina motion to table the Foster report from passing. Then northerners gladly accepted Madison's key amendment to the Foster report that removed any ambiguity in the key section that some thought implied congressional power of emancipation after 1808 by rewording it to say "that Congress have no authority to interfere in the emancipation of slaves, or in the treatment of them." Just as at the Constitutional Convention of 1787, where the desire of northern delegates for investing the federal government with the power to regulate commerce by simple majority vote in Congress had been traded for their acquiescence to the South on the slave-trade and fugitive-slave clauses, now the northern representatives were unwilling to jeopardize funding and assumption by offending representatives from the lower South. It was a matter, as John Pemberton put it, of "scratch me and I will scratch thee."[48] Most northern congressmen claimed to be antislavery, but their commitment evaporated when it reached the point where the material interests of their states became involved. Oliver Wolcott, the Connecticut Federalist, captured the position of most northern congressmen when he wrote to his son in the spring of 1790 that he favored "the white people of this country to the black—after they [Congress] have taken care of the former they may amuse themselves with the other people."[49]

The Social Question

Within a few months of the revealing congressional debate over slavery in 1790 and at a time when the North and South had learned to reconcile their differences over the management of the western lands, a prominent Virginian published a plan for a gradual emancipation. Ferdinando Fairfax, a protege of George Washington and a man with many ties to Virginia's planter aristocracy, argued that many slaveholders were ready to release their slaves voluntarily and many others could be induced to do so with compensation. But Virginians, argued Fairfax, vehemently resisted the idea of having freed slaves in their midst and would never admit of equal privileges for those whom they emancipated. Hence, gradual abolition must be accompanied by recolonization in Africa, Fairfax suggested (as

42

had Thomas Jefferson in 1776) under the auspices of the federal government. Fairfax's plan was notable not only in pointing to a widespread desire among Virginians (who represented about half of the nation's slaveowners) to be quit of slavery but the simultaneous desire to be quit of blacks.[50] It was a desire, as it turned out, widely shared by northerners.

It is telling that no discussion in the North found its way into public prints after this southern proposal for a federally sponsored gradual abolition. Fairfax's plan was not unknown to northerners, for he published it not in Virginia but in Philadelphia, in Mathew Carey's *American Museum*, the most widely subscribed magazine of the early federal period. Fairfax's conclusions about the sentiment against free blacks living among whites was ominous, for thousands of Virginia slaves had by now been liberated, and white sentiment, in the North as well as the South, was beginning to turn against them. A general emancipation, northerners had reason to believe, would bring free blacks churning northward in search of economic opportunity and some measure of social justice.

Six years later, in 1796, another prominent Virginian laid before the legislature of his state another plan for the gradual abolition of slavery. Much had transpired since the first Congress had buried the issue of slavery. But two occurrences weighed with special force upon the mind of St. George Tucker, a prominent lawyer and state officeholder. First, was the emerging knowledge of a demographic explosion revealed by the first federal census in 1790; the second was a political explosion that had erupted in the Caribbean shortly after the census of 1790 was taken. Both frightened Tucker, for together they seemed to spell the ruination of the South.

Tucker reported that the first federal census showed that nearly 293,000 slaves resided in Virginia—roughly a 250 percent increase since 1755 and an increase of more than a third since 1782, despite the flight of thousands of slaves to the British during the Revolution, the migration of many freed slaves to the North after the war, and the sale of a large number of slaves southward in the 1780s. In the Tidewater, enslaved blacks now constituted more than 50 percent of the population.[51] Alarmingly, instead of withering, as many expected after Virginia had halted slave importations in 1774, slavery was growing rapidly.

Tucker clothed his appeal for gradual abolition on precisely the point that had been made repeatedly during the revolutionary period—that the institution was incompatible with republican government and was a monstrous stain on the national escutcheon. But the timing of his proposal—and his hopes for its success—rested far more on the widespread fear that black rebellion on the French sugar-producing island of St. Domingue had aroused throughout the South. Partly inspired by the American Revolution, a black revolt had broken out on the French island in 1791. In the next few years it produced spiraling racial violence and wholesale killing and had sent thousands of French planters fleeing to the American mainland, many with slaves in tow. The volcanic fury of the enslaved Caribbean masses shook many whites to their boots, including some abolitionists.[52] In Virginia, where many refugees came with their slaves, fear spread that the revolt might touch off a sister insurrection. "The calamities which have lately spread like a contagion through the West India islands," Tucker wrote to a friend in Massachusetts, "afford a solemn warning to us of the dangerous predicament in which we stand. . . ."[53]

Certain that the demographic history of Virginia was paralleling that of the French West Indies in a way that made massive black rebellion a near certainty, Tucker summoned history and the principles of the Revolution to convince his countrymen of the need for immediate action. Tucker began by quoting Montesquieu's powerful words from the title page of *Spirit of the Laws*: "Slavery not only violates the Laws of Nature, and of civil Society, it also wounds the best Forms of Government; in a Democracy, where all Men are equal, Slavery is contrary to the Spirit of the Constitution." Then Tucker provided readers with a capsule history of slavery in the New World, organized around the point that "Whilst America hath been the land of promise to Europeans, and their descendants, it hath been the vale of death to millions of the wretched sons of Africa. The genial light of liberty, which hath here shone with unrivalled lustre on the former, hath yielded no comfort to the latter, but to them hath proved a pillar of darkness."[54]

Tucker excused the men of '76 for their inability to deal with the wretched institution "during the convulsions of a revolution," but he argued that now, in a state of "constitutional health and vigour," Americans must remove the "stigma" of slavery in order to uphold "the principles of our government, and of that revolution upon which it is founded."[55] That such a "horrid practice" as the slave trade could be "sanctioned by a civilized nation" was a national disgrace; "that a nation ardent in the cause of liberty . . . can continue to vindicate a right established upon such a foundation" was a national disgrace; "that a people who have declared, 'That *all men* are by nature *equally free* and *independent*,' and have made this declaration the first article in the foundation of their government, should in defiance of so sacred a truth, . . . tolerate a practice incompatible therewith" was a national disgrace.[56]

Like Ferdinando Fairfax, Tucker designed his publication with northerners as well as southerners in mind and may have even designed it as an invitation to the North. While preparing his plan for gradual abolition, Tucker had corresponded with Jeremy Belknap, one of Boston's leading Congregational ministers, regarding the ending of slavery in Virginia. Belknap had queried a number of prominent friends in trying to help Tucker find a formula for abolition. Tucker judged that an abolition of slavery in Virginia was by no means impossible. "A large majority of slave-holders among us," he told Belknap, "would cheerfully concur in any feasible plan for the abolition of it [slavery]"[57] That this was no wild opinion is indicated by Tuck-

er's willingness to state publicly in the pamphlet of the following year that it is "unquestionably true, that a very large
proportion of our fellow-citizens lament [slavery] as a misfortune."[58] Within a few months, echoing Tucker, Jefferson
wrote that "if something is not done, and done soon, we shall
be the murderers of our own children . . . ; the revolutionary
storm, now sweeping the globe, will be upon us."[59]

Tucker's plan is important because it was, in its way, another plea to the North to assist in the work of dismantling
slavery and because it went beyond Fairfax's plan in offering
more concrete proposals for eliminating the two obstacles that
had heretofore impeded progress on this issue—the economic
interest of slaveholders and the deeply rooted feeling among
whites that blacks were so inferior that they could not be
incorporated into white society on an equal footing. Tucker
specifically pointed to these as the most important objections
of "most others [plans] that have been submitted to the consideration of the public. . . ."[60] Tucker thought he could over-
come the economic question by granting liberty to female slaves
born after a certain date only after they had reached 28 years
of age, thus allowing masters to recapture their investment, and
by requiring even the male and female children of these black
women born free to serve 28 years.[61] His plan, in other words,
would be cost-free to the present generation of slaveowners
and required not a penny of northerners in taxes or appro-
priations from the government's general fund.

To the second problem Tucker had a harsh solution,
though less harsh than the forced colonization in Africa that
Fairfax had proposed. Spreading abolition over nearly 100 years,
he argued, would allow blacks to acquire skills and behavioral
patterns that would make them more acceptable to whites; but
even so he doubted that white Virginians would find them
acceptable, and so they were to be excluded from most civil
rights or liberties, including voting, officeholding, owning land,
keeping arms, intermarrying with whites, serving as witness

The Failure of Abolitionism

or juror in cases involving whites, and even making a will or testament. Thus would blacks, given legal freedom but kept in social bondage, be driven to emigrate voluntarily to uninhabited western lands or to the Spanish territories in Florida and Louisiana.

Tucker's *Dissertation on Slavery* could not have escaped the attention of northern political leaders because it too was published in Philadelphia where Congress was now sitting; it is even possible that Tucker chose to have it published in that city in order to put it squarely before their view. But Tucker, like other prominent Virginians concerned to find a way of disengaging from slavery, could evoke no response from northern leaders. Even the Quaker-led Pennsylvania Abolition Society, perhaps stung by the failure of their attempts in 1790 to get congressional action, failed to suggest or promote a plan of emancipation carried out under the auspices of the national government. In fact the PAS, when it had the opportunity, refused even to seek the judicial abolition of slavery in Pennsylvania, though precedent for this had been provided in Massachusetts in 1786.

Following the disclosure of Gabriel Prosser's intended general insurrection in Virginia in 1800, Virginians, as well as southerners farther south, had further reason to tremble at the demon in their midst and thought again about emancipation. St. George Tucker's cousin, George Tucker, took up the cudgels in 1801 in an anonymous pamphlet that called slavery "an eating sore" and "this growing evil." Tucker predicted that the growing literacy of blacks in the state would increase their appetite for freedom—a hunger he called "this celestial spark" and "an inborn sentiment, which the God of nature has planted deep in the heart."[62] Hence, he warned, Virginians could expect only greater unrest among their captive labor force. By this time, George Tucker had nearly given up appealing to conscience. He would pass by the appeal to "the duty we owe them as creatures made by the same hand, and in the same mould as ourselves," he wrote, and merely mention the old refrain that slavery was inconsistent "with the truest principles of republicanism."[63] Instead, his main appeal was to the self-interest of his fellow Virginians, to their instinct for self-preservation. Tucker also gave up the idea that freedmen could be incorporated, even if only very gradually, into white republican society. He advocated their release and immediate removal to the western lands—far from the South and far from the North as well.

As the Jeffersonian presidency proceeded after 1800, it became apparent that the time had nearly passed when a gradual but general emancipation might have worked. The environmentalist belief of the Revolutionary period posited that circumstances, not inborn qualities, accounted for the degradation of Africans in America was weakening, with the old view that blacks were innately inferior making a resurgence. Free blacks were more and more regarded as a dangerous element, to be controlled or excluded from society. Moreover, the economic viability of slavery had suddenly been greatly enhanced by Eli Whitney's famous invention. As before, no northerners came forward with emancipation schemes, nor did they tender support for those that southerners continued to put before the public.

In 1803, the year that the St. Dominguan revolution culminated in the final defeat of white French colonialism, St. George Tucker republished his plan, again in Philadelphia.[64] A New Jersey congressman proposed gradual emancipation for slaves in the District of Columbia in the same year.[65] In 1810, two southerners, the Maryland Quaker John Parrish and the abolitionist Lewis Dupre put forward plans, both variations on the formula of emancipation followed by removal.[66] Madison would make a last-ditch attempt, as the question of extending slavery into Missouri and Kansas heated up, with his gradual emancipation proposal in 1819, by which time he estimated that $240 million would be required to settle freed blacks on western lands. In 1824, two years before he died, Jefferson proposed a federally financed plan for gradual abolition, and in the next year the English reformer Fanny Wright put forward another plan.[67]

And by this time, opinion had turned strongly against the thousands of free blacks who had sought a life of freedom in the northern cities. Any ember of northern desire to participate in a national plan for abolition, gradual or immediate, had ceased to glow. Instead, a belligerent white supremacism was manifesting itself throughout the North. As early as 1805, white Philadelphians drove their black neighbors from the traditional Fourth of July celebrations in Independence Square. Within another decade the first burning of a black northern church took place in the City of Brotherly Love.[68]

The rampaging white racism that developed in the aftermath of the War of 1812 took institutional form in the American Colonization Society, founded in 1817 and dedicated both to Christianizing slaves and to shipping free blacks back to Africa. At a lower level, in urban streets, hostility against free blacks took the form of bloody attacks on black neighborhoods. Northern whites began demonstrating militantly that they had little commitment to a biracial republic. The republican edifice they were constructing would provide little shelter to those who were black—free or slave. Slavery would remain a national problem, not a southern problem, but northerners, with few exceptions, acknowledged no responsibility for solving the problem. In fact, many within the northern intellectual elite, including such titans of northern academic training as Timothy Dwight and Samuel Stanhope Smith, president of Yale and Princeton respectively in the early nineteenth century, helped to forge "a new framework for the discussion of slavery"—a framework, as Larry Tise has shown, upon which an "antebellum proslavery tradition" could be built.[69] Conservative northern Federalists, not southerners, "were the first Americans to revive the defense of slavery in public" in the second

49

decade of the nineteenth century. With northerners becoming increasingly involved in the booming cotton economy of the South, such former officers of the Pennsylvania Abolition Society as Tench Coxe were publishing virulently racist essays denying that free blacks, as well as Native Americans and other people of color, were genetically endowed for citizenship.[70]

From failing to support abolition plans put forward by southerners in the 1780s and 1790s to their emergence in the first quarter of the nineteenth century as contrivers of an intellectual defense of slavery, northern leaders—political, academic, and clerical—consistently ducked the issue that the Revolutionary leaders had insisted must be solved if the nation was to be united and true to the sacred texts enunciated during its birth. Slavery would continue to grow in the South and the problem of slavery would continue to require a national solution. When it came, the solution was so costly that the casualty rate was more than five times as great as Americans sustained in World War II. The North has always blamed the South for that carnage from 1861 to 1865, but in truth the North was equally blameworthy.

NOTES

1. Paul Finkelman, "Slavery and the Constitutional Convention: Making a Covenant with Death," in Richard Beeman, Stephen Botein, and Edward C. Carter II, eds., *Beyond Confederation: Origins of the Constitution and American National Identity* (Chapel Hill, N. C., 1987), 193.

2. *The Federalist*, ed. Jacob E. Cooke (Middletown, Conn., 1961), 594.

3. Luther Martin, "Genuine Information," Baltimore *Maryland Gazette*, Jan. 22, 1788, in John P. Kaminski and Gaspare J. Saladino, eds., *Commentaries on the Constitution* (Madison, Wis., 1981–), XV, 433; "Genuine Information," Baltimore *Maryland Gazette*, Jan. 18, 1788, ibid., 414.

4. Drew R. McCoy, *The Last of the Fathers: James Madison and the Republican Legacy* (Cambridge, Mass., 1989), passim and especially ch. 7.

5. "John Adams' Notes of Debate," July 30, 1776, Paul H. Smith, ed., *Letters of Delegates to Congress* (Washington, D. C., 1976—), IV, 568; Rutledge quoted in Finkelman, *Beyond Confederation*, 214.

6. Randolph C. Downes, "Creek-American Relations, 1782–1790," *Georgia Historical Quarterly*, 21 (1937), 162–63; Arthur Preston Whitaker, "Alexander McGillivray, 1783–1789," *North Carolina Historical Review*, 5 (1928), 198.

7. George Washington to Samuel Powel, Jan. 18, 1788, *Commentaries on the Constitution*, XV, 399.

8. *Annals of Congress*, 1 Cong., 1 Sess., 70, 696–703.

9. For a general treatment of the sectional controversies in the 1780s, see Joseph L. Davis, *Sectionalism in American Politics, 1774–1787* (Madison, Wis., 1977), passim and especially chs. 5–6; John P. Kaminski, et al., eds., *The Documentary History of the Ratification of the Constitution* (Madison, Wis., 1976—), XIII, 27, 33–34. For the rumor of the severing of South Carolina and Georgia from the other states in a proposed peace treaty see James Lovell to Samuel Adams, March 17, 1780, Smith, *Letters of Delegates to Congress, XIV,* 514–15, and the pamphlet by the Georgia delegates to Congress, *Observations upon the Effect of Certain Late Political Suggestions* . . . (Philadelphia, 1781). I am indebted to John Kaminski for these references.

10. James Monroe to Patrick Henry, Aug. 12, 1786, quoted in Staughton Lynd, *Class Conflict, Slavery, and the United States Constitution* (Indianapolis, 1967), 171.

11. Tench Coxe, "Letter from Tench Coxe, esq. to the Commissioners of the state of Virginia at the Annapolis Convention," Philadelphia *American Museum*, 7 (June 1790), 293–94.

12. How this occurred in Pennsylvania, the first northern state to pass a gradual abolition law, is examined in Gary B. Nash and Jean R. Soderlund, *Freedom by Degrees: Emancipation and its Aftermath in Pennsylvania* (New York, 1990).

13. Madison to Robert J. Evans, June 15, 1819, *Letters and Other Writings of James Madison* (4 vols.; Philadelphia, 1865), III, 135.

14. Jefferson to Richard Price, Aug. 7, 1785, Julian P. Boyd et al., eds., *The Papers of Thomas Jefferson* (Princeton, N. J., 1950—), VIII, 357.

15. Allison to Ezra Stiles, Oct. 20, 1768, quoted in Winthrop Jordan, *White Over Black: American Attitudes Toward the Negro, 1550–1812* (Chapel Hill, N. C., 1968), 299.

16. Nash and Soderlund, *Freedom by Degrees*, ch. 5.

17. Rush, *Address on Slave-Keeping*, 30, quoted in Jordan, *White Over Black*, 300–1.

18. Rush to Sharp, May 1, 1773, Lyman H. Butterfield, ed., *The Letters of Benjamin Rush* (2 vols.; Princeton, N. J., 1951), I, 81.

19. Rush to Julia Rush, July 23, 1776, ibid., I, 106.

20. Rush to Sharp, Nov. 28, 1783, John A. Woods, ed., "The Correspondence of Benjamin Rush and Granville Sharp, 1773–1809," *Journal of American Studies*, 1 (1967), 20.

21. Rush, "Paradise of Negro Slaves," in *Essays, Literary, Moral, and Philosophical* (Philadelphia, 1798), 315–20.

22. Rush to Belknap, Aug. 18, 178, in *Letters of Rush*, I, 482–83.

23. Mathew Ridley to Miss Livingston, n.d., quoted in Duncan J. McLeod, *Slavery, Race and the American Revolution* (Cambridge, 1974), 75.

24. Edward Needles, *An Historical Memoir of the Pennsylvania Society for Promoting the Abolition of Slavery . . .* (Philadelphia, 1848), 23.

25. Robert Fogel and Stanley Engerman, "Philanthropy at Bargain Prices: Notes on the Economics of Gradual Emancipation," *Journal of Legal Studies*, 3 (1974), 380–81.

26. *Pennsylvania Gazette*, Feb. 2, 1780; Fogel and Engerman, "Philanthropy at Bargain Prices," 401.

27. "A Farmer" [David Cooper], "To the Publick," *New Jersey Journal*, Sept. 20, 1780.

28. Morris, quoted in Finkelman, "Slavery and the Constitutional Convention," 212.

29. Peter S. Onuf, "Liberty, Development, and Union: Visons of the West in the 1780s," *William and Mary Quarterly*, 3d ser., 43 (1986), 208.

30. Webster, *Political Essays on the Nature and Operations of Money, Public Finances, and Other Subjects* (Philadelphia, 1791), 488, 490.

31. Benjamin Horace Hibbard, *A History of the Public Land Policies* (New York, 1939), 55, 100.

32. Onuf, "Liberty, Development, and Union," 181.

33. The petitions are in *Annals of Congress*, 1 Cong., 2 Sess., 1182–84 and 1197–98.

34. The fullest analysis of the debate is Howard A. Ohline, "Slavery, Economics, and Congressional Politics, 1790," *Journal of Southern History*, 46 (1980), 335–60. The three newspapers were *The Gazette of the United States* (Philadelphia), the New York *Daily Advertiser*, and the *New York Daily Gazette*.

35. Thomas Lloyd, "Reports on the First Federal Congress," (transcriptions from Lloyd's shorthand notes), II, 120, Documentary History of the First Federal Congress, George Washington University, Washington, D. C.; *Annals of Congress*, 1 Cong., 2 Sess., 1240–47.

36. Ibid.

37. Coxe to James Madison, March 31, 1790, Robert A. Rutland et al., eds., *The Papers of James Madison* (Chicago, Ill. and Charlottesville, Va., 1962–) XIII, 132.

38. Pennsylvania Abolition Society broadside, Nov. 9, 1789, PAS Papers, Historical Society of Pennsylvania, Philadelphia; PAS petition of Feb. 12, 1790, in *Annals of Congress*, 1 Cong., 2 Sess., 1197–98.

39. Ohline, "Slavery, Economics, and Congressional Politics," 346.

40. The committee report is in Linda Grant DePauw et al., eds., *Documentary History of the First Federal Congress of the United States of America* (Baltimore, 1972–), III, 340–41.

41. Ohline, "Slavery, Economics, and Congressional Politics," 346.

42. New York *Daily Advertiser*, March 20, 1790.

43. *New York Daily Gazette*, March 22, 1790.

44. Philadelphia *Freeman's Journal*, Aug. 11, 1790, "Extract of a letter from a gentleman in Charleston, (S. C.) to his friend in New-Jersey, dated March 31 [1790]."

45. Madison to Edmund Randolph, March 21, 1790, *The Papers of James Madison*, XIII, 110; Madison to Benjamin Rush, March 20, 1790, ibid., 109. The long series of letters from John Pemberton to his brother James, an officer of the Pennsylvania Abolition Society, is in the Papers of the Pennsylvania Abolition Society, Historical

Society of Pennsylvania. The letters are dated March 8, 9, 14, 16, 17, 18, 20, and 23, 1790.

46. Ohline, "Slavery, Economics, and Congressional Politics," 349.

47. John Pemberton to James Pemberton, March 16, 1790, PAS Papers, HSP.

48. John Pemberton to James Pemberton, Feb. 23, 1790, PAS Papers, HSP.

49. Oliver Wolcott, Sr., to Oliver Wolcott, Jr., April 23, 1790, quoted in Ohline, "Slavery, Economics, and Congressional Politics," 354.

50. "Plan for Liberating the Negroes within the United States," Philadelphia *American Museum*, VIII (Dec., 1790), 285–87.

51. St. George Tucker, *A Dissertation on Slavery: With a Proposal for the Gradual Abolition of It, in the State of Virginia* (Philadelphia, 1796), 40. (See Documents, p. 154.)

52. Alfred N. Hunt, *Haiti's Influence on Antebellum America* (Baton Rouge, La., 1988).

53. Tucker to Jeremy Belknap, June 29, 1795, in Massachusetts Historical Society *Collections*, 5th ser. (Boston, 1877), III, 406.

54. Tucker, *Dissertation on Slavery*, 9. (See Documents, p. 152.)

55. Ibid., 11. (See Documents, pp. 153–53.)

56. Ibid., 27–30. (See Documents, p. 156.) Tucker was quoting Article 1 of the Virginia Declaration of Rights.

57. Tucker to Belknap, June 29, 1795, Mass. Hist. Soc. *Collections*, III, 407.

58. Tucker, *Dissertation on Slavery*, 67. (see Documents, p. 154.)

59. Jefferson to St. George Tucker, Aug. 28, 1797, *Writings of Thomas Jefferson*, Andrew Lipscomb and Albert Bergh, eds. (20 vols.; Washington, D. C., 1903), IX, 418.

60. Tucker, *Dissertation on Slavery*, 8.

61. Ibid., 91–94. (See Documents, p. 155–56.)

62. George Tucker, *A Letter to a Member of the General Assembly of Virginia, on the Subject of the Late Conspiracy of the Slaves, with a Proposal for their Colonization* (Richmond, Va., 1801), 5–6. (See Documents, p. 161.)

63. Ibid., 19–20.

64. Tucker, *Blackstone's Commentaries: With Notes of Reference, to the Constitution* ... (Philadelphia, 1803), I, pt. II, 31–85.

65. *Annals of Congress*, 8 Cong., 2 Sess., 995–96.

66. Parrish, *Remarks on the Slavery of the Black People: Addressed to the Citizens of the United States* ... (Philadelphia, 1806); Dupre, *A Rational and Benevolent Plan for Averting Some of the Calamitous Consequences of Slavery, Being a Practicable, Seasonable, and Profitable Institution for the Progressive Emancipation of Virginia and Carolina Slaves* (n.p., 1810).

67. Thomas Jefferson to Jared Sparks, Feb. 4, 1824, Merrill D. Peterson, ed., *Thomas Jefferson Writings* (New York, 1984), 1484–87; Celia Morris Eckhardt, *Fanny Wright: Rebel in America* (Cambridge, Mass., 1984), ch. 5.

68. Gary B. Nash, *Forging Freedom: The Formation of Philadelphia's Black Community, 1720–1840* (Cambridge, Mass., 1988), 213.

69. Larry E. Tise, *Proslavery: A History of the Defense of Slavery in America, 1701–1840* (Athens, Ga., 1987), ch. 8.

70. Ibid., 228–29.

Russian diplomat Paul Svinin painted this street scene in
Philadelphia during his American tour, 1811–1813. Juxtaposed
are the great white facade of the Bank of Philadelphia and
a group of free black laborers, who played an important, but
not often noticed, role in the new nation's economy. *The
Metropolitam Museum of Art, Rogers Fund, 1942. (42.95.16)
All rights reserved.*

THREE

Black Americans in a White Republic

IT IS FITTING THAT THE STRUGGLE to launch the independent American republic has attracted the attention of hundreds of historians over the last two centuries and that the history of particular communities, social groups, and individuals has been traced with loving care. Yet few historians have studied the revolutionary experience of African-Americans.[1] And we still lack a proper appreciation of the emergence of an African-American leadership group, forged on the anvil of revolutionary struggles for freedom. This group was faced in the postrevolutionary era with the dual task of creating the institutions of free black life in the North and upper South and fighting against slavery and racism as they grew more powerful and spread geographically after ratification of the Constitution. Neglect of the black freedom struggles that occurred in revolutionary and postrevolutionary America has turned the African-American fifth of the population into a far more passive group than it actually was. In reality, the American Revolution represents the largest slave uprising in our history. Moreover, in the aftermath of Revolution, when thousands of slaves obtained their freedom, free blacks laid down the foundations of black institutional life in the North and, at the same time, dealt with the reality, obvious soon after the new federal government was in place, that slavery was not going to wither in the United States.

Slaves in the American colonies were not directly affected by revenue stamps, sugar duties, or tea parties; nonetheless they were politicized by the language and modes of white protest and were quick to seize the opportunities for securing their freedom that emerged from the disruptions of a society in rebellion. Working in taverns and coffeehouses where revolutionary politics were hatched, eavesdropping on their masters' dinner table conversations, and in some cases actually reading newspapers and pamphlets containing white protests against slavery, blacks imbibed the ideology of natural and inalienable rights and fit the ringing phrases of the day to their own situation. "In every human breast," the young Phillis Wheatley wrote from Boston, "God has implanted a Principle, which we call love of freedom; it is impatient of Oppression, and pants for Deliverance; and by the leave of our modern Egyptians I will assert, that the same Principle lives in us."[2] The reference to Egyptians was a poignant stroke, for it identified the liberty-craving Americans, who since the founding generation in New England had seen themselves as oppressed Israelites fleeing into Canaan, the Promised Land. In this way, enslaved black Americans became the Chosen People for whom God had special purposes.

In various towns of the North, slaves acted on their impatience with oppression, petitioning for their freedom in ways calculated to prick the conscience of the master class. "Let slave behaviour be what it will," admonished Felix of Boston in 1773, the first slave in America to petition a legislature for the abolition of slavery, "neither they, nor their Children to all Generations, shall ever be able to do, or to possess and enjoy any Thing, no, not even *Life itself*, but in a Manner as the *Beasts that perish*." Holbrook pleaded that emancipation "to

us will be as Life from the dead."³ Acting very little like quiescent Sambos, slaves couched their petitions cautiously at first
but became bolder as the war began. They made indelibly clear
that they did not regard their requests for freedom as appeals
to a merciful master class but as a demand for the restoration
of inherent rights unlawfully wrested from them. "We expect
your house [the legislature] will . . . take our deplorable case
into serious consideration, and give us that ample relief which,
as men, we have a natural right to," remonstrated four slaves
in Thompson, Massachusetts. Six years later, in 1779, blacks in
Connecticut echoed these thoughts: "We do ask for nothing,
but what we are fully persuaded is ours to claim," remonstrated
two Connecticut slaves in 1779, for "Reason and Revelation
join to declare, that we are the Creatures of that God, who
made of one Blood, and Kindred, all the Nations of the Earth
. . . there is nothing that leads us to a Belief, or Suspicion,
that we are any more obliged to serve them, than they us, and
the more we Consider of this matter, the more we are Convinced of our Right . . . to be free . . . and can never be convinced that we were made to be Slaves."⁴ Such statements,
denying their inferiority, proclaiming the universality of all
mankind, and throwing the political theory being fashioned to
justify the American challenge against English oppression in
the face of American patriots, provide some of the most compelling language of the revolutionary era.

By its very nature the revolutionary war created wholly
new situations for slaves. With the gigantic movement of both
civilian and military populations in and out of nearly every
major seaport city from Savannah to Boston between 1775 and
1781, urban slaves had unprecedented opportunities for making
their personal declarations of independence. Similarly, in the
countryside, as Tory and Whig militia units criss-crossed the
terrain, plundering the estates of their enemies, slaves found
ways of tearing gaping holes in the fabric of slavery. Discov-
ering the power of the revolutionary ideology of protest, slaves

found the greatest opportunities for applying it by fleeing to the very forces against which Americans directed their ideological barbs. Whereas the Americans would only occasionally offer freedom for blacks serving in place of their masters, the British made it general policy to offer liberty to any escaped slave. In the North, where the war centered for most of the first five years, this led to a general sympathy among African-Americans for the British cause. As the German Lutheran leader Henry Melchior Muhlenberg noted, blacks "secretly wished the British army might win, for then all Negro slaves will gain their freedom."[5] Thus did a New York slave become "Torified like most of your colour," according to a patriot in Crevecoeur's *Sketches*.[6]

In the North and South, thousands of slaves fled whenever the British forces were within reach. Although the number can never be exactly calculated, it was very large. Jefferson reported that 30,000 slaves had fled their masters during the British invasion of Virginia in 1781.[7] Knowing that more than half of Virginia's blacks were in situations that would have made flight nearly unthinkable—because they were children under 15, physically depleted men and women over 45, women with young children, or men whose flight would have left their families at the mercy of revengeful masters—this is a gigantic number, probably representing about half of what we might call "eligible" escapees, predominantly male. In South Carolina, a similar proportion of adult males—about half—probably fled to the British during the southern campaigns from 1779 to 1781.[8] In eastern Pennsylvania, where slavery existed in a milder form than in the South, the flight from slavery reached similar proportions. "By the invasion of this state, and the possession the enemy obtained of this city, and neighbourhood," wrote the wartime leader, George Bryan of Philadelphia, in 1779, "[a] great part of the slaves hereabouts, were enticed away by the British army."[9]

In New York City and its surrounding hinterland in New York and northern New Jersey, which contained some 15,000 slaves, the largest urban concentration in the colonies, the run-away rate jumped hugely during the war years. The slave of Quaker John Corlies is illustrative. Named Titus by his master, this 21-year-old fled his owner in 1775 and fled south to join the black regiments being formed by Virginia's royal governor, Lord Dunmore. A year later, Titus, renaming himself Colonel Tye, was back in northern New Jersey organizing other slaves and free blacks to fight against the Americans. For five years, he served as the leader of a local guerilla band that terrorized the patriot farms of northern New Jersey. Tye, known as "one of Lord Dunmore's Crew," fought his own American Revolution for five years before dying from battle wounds and lock-jaw.[10]

However, it was not those who sought their freedom by fighting with the British who would become the root stock of postwar black society. Thousands of slaves who fled to the British died of camp fever, malnutrition, and battle wounds, and among the black Loyalists who survived the war, most were evacuated in 1783 to Florida, Jamaica, and Nova Scotia. By dint of this exodus, the African-American part of society lost a great many of the most physically vigorous, psychologically aggressive, and politically able of its half million members. Emerging from the war, the African-American population must have included a disproportionate number of older slaves, women with small children, and those physically broken or emotionally paralyzed by the slave experience.

Yet in spite of the heavy losses of black males in the prime of life, vigorous and visionary free black communities began to form throughout the North in the immediate postwar years. The largest were in maritime towns because that was where work and companionship were most available. But hardly any sizeable town between Maine and Maryland failed to develop a subcommunity of free blacks, each with men and women who emerged as leaders of one kind or another. By looking at several of these leaders we can see some of the pathways that led from the denial of autonomy under slavery to creative, though often obstructed, roles under freedom.

Jupiter Hammon of Long Island can be taken as an example of the most cautious, tentative yearning for freedom that developed during the war. Born a slave in 1711 near Oyster Bay on Long Island Sound to the prominent Lloyd family of merchants and manorial landlords, Hammon served as a valued house servant. Early converted to Christianity, Hammon wrote poetry filled with ecstatic yearnings for salvation in the afterlife. When the Lloyds fled Long Island for Connecticut after the British occupied New York City in 1776, Hammon, already 65 years old, willingly stayed at their side rather than flee to the British lines, as so many New York slaves were doing. Even accused of petitioning the Connecticut legislature against abolishing slavery, a charge he emphatically denied, Hammon continued to preach the gospel of the redeeming salvation that would come to those, black and white alike, who accepted Christ. "If we are slaves it is by the permission of God; if we are free it must be by the power of the most high God. . . ."[11]

However, even in Hammon, who would seem the most quiescent of slaves, largely unaffected by the cracks in the wall of slavery that had appeared during the Revolution, sparks of the freedom fighter smoldered. In 1782, for example, in "A Winter Piece," he called for the moral reformation of African-Americans and exhorted them, as Philip Richards has shown, "to assert themselves as a nation within a nation, retaining their African identity while continuing to exist within American society."[12] After the war, Hammon maintained a distinctly gradualist approach to the condition of most of the new nation's blacks who remained in slavery. But he chided white Americans to the end. His last published piece, written when he was 76 years old, was *An Address to the Negroes In the State of New-York* published as the Constitutional Convention was gathering in Philadelphia. In this essay, Hammon wrote that Africans, "from our own feelings," knew that liberty was a priceless attribute. Its value was evident in "the conduct of the white people in the late war. How much money has been spent, and how many lives have been lost to defend their liberty!" Hammon confided that he had "hoped that God would open their eyes, when they were so much engaged for liberty, to think of the state of the poor blacks, and pity them." But they had done so only in small measure. What might now be done? "This, my dear brethren," Hammon counseled some 50,000 slaves in the state of New York, "is by no means the greatest thing we have to be concerned about. Getting our liberty in this world is nothing to our having the liberty of the children of God. . . . What is forty, fifty, or sixty years, when compared to eternity?"[13]

Hammon had found his peace and, as he said, "must soon to the way of all the earth."[14] But in the new nation other African-Americans had whole lifetimes ahead of them. The human material out of which postwar black society would have to be constructed included many who were less cautious than Hammon. Yet some of them had played their hands carefully during the war because they already had secured a small stake in American society. Some had thrown in their lot with a patriot society whose rhetoric of natural rights and personal freedom gave them hopes for the end of slavery and the dawn of a new era. Such a man was James Forten of Philadelphia.

According to family history, Forten's great-grandfather had been brought to the Delaware River Valley in chains, probably by the Dutch, even before William Penn's Quakers arrived. Forten's grandfather must have been one of the first blacks in Pennsylvania to purchase his freedom. His son became a free black sailmaker, and into his family James had been born in 1766. As a youth, James Forten had attended Anthony Benezet's school where the kindly Quaker taught him to read and write and to believe in the universality of humankind. In 1781, as the war was winding down, the 15-year-old Forten signed as a powderboy on Stephen Decatur's privateer, the *Royal Louis*.

His father had died recently, and the family was in need. Decatur's venture was finanaced in part by Robert Bridges, who employed James's father for many years in his sailloft, and thus was the young free black Philadelphian placed with Decatur. As it happened, this launched a career punctuated by heroic acts that would make Forten one of Philadelphia's most notable citizens. When the *Royal Louis* was captured by a British ship after a fierce battle at sea, Forten was befriended by the British captain's young son. But the black Philadelphia lad refused free passage to England and the patronage of the ship's captain. "NO, NO!" he was later reported to have cried, "I am here a prisoner for the liberties of my country; I never, NEVER, shall prove a traitor to her interests."[15] Sent to a death-trap prison ship anchored in New York harbor, Forten was released at war's end and made his way shoeless from New York back to his home town.

Taking up his father's trade, Forten became a highly successful sailmaker, with white and black journeyman toiling in his sail loft on the Delaware River waterfront. Such was his respect in the white community that wealthy Philadelphia merchants, whose ships were outfitted with the carefully cut sails from Forten's loft, attended his wedding in the early nineteenth century. But part of this respect was based on Forten's avoidance of controversy or any act that the white community might regard as presumptuous. When Philadelphia's first black organization was forming in 1786, the Free African Society of Philadelphia, Forten was not among those who chose to join. A few years later, when a number of free blacks laid plans for the first independent black church, Forten was not among them, although he was climbing rapidly to success by then as a sailmaker. White leaders, including some who had been supporting the emerging community of free blacks, reacted strongly against what they regarded as arrogance among so humble and inferior a people who presumed to build their own religious institution; but Forten could not have come in for any blame because he had chosen not to participate. Not until 1797 did he emerge from the shadows, joining nearly 80 of the city's blacks in a petition to Congress against the slave trade. From then on, his place secure in Philadelphia, he became an outspoken leader of the black community.[16]

Like Forten, Prince Hall of Boston had secured a small stake in American society by the outbreak of the Revolution, and that kept him faithful to the American cause. But unlike Forten, he emerged from the war as a resolute organizer of free blacks. Black Americans, he believed, would never gain more than a glimpse of freedom, would never move beyond a hollow legal freedom to a place of dignity and equality in American life, unless they organized themselves to cope with the uncaring or hostile white world around them. The slave of William Hall, a Boston merchant, Prince Hall was about 40 years old when the Revolution broke out. Since 1762, he had worshiped at the School Street Church shepherded by the radical awakener Andrew Crosswell, who had preached against slavery since the 1740s when he emerged as one of the most effective New Light preachers in the Boston area. Hall had received his freedom in 1770, and it seems probable that a few years later he played a role in the five petitions that Boston's blacks placed before the legislature between 1773 and 1775. Several of these remonstrances against slavery came from a group of fourteen black Masons, Hall among them, who had joined a Masonic lodge formed by one of the British regiments in the town. "We expect great things from men who have made such a noble stand against the designs of their *fellow-men* to enslave them," read one petition. Another pointed to the contradiction of those "held in a state of slavery, within the bowels of a free Country"; while a third declared that "we have in common with all other men a natural right to our freedoms . . . as we are a freeborn people and have never forfeited this blessing by any compact or agreement whatever."[17]

When the war began, Hall kept up his campaign against slavery. As the British were evacuating Boston, they gave Hall permission to establish a separate black Masonic lodge, and four of its members, including Hall, were among eight black petitioners in 1777 who implored the legislature to abolish slavery, restore "the Natural Rights of all men," and thus remove the "inconsistancy of acting themselves the part which they condemn and oppose in others."[18] Their pleas were answered within a few years as the supreme court of the Commonwealth decided that nothing in the Massachusetts constitution justified slavery, and the bill of rights forbade it.

The fires that burned in Hall never subsided in the postwar period. But Boston's black community had much to suffer. While slavery was abolished by judicial decree in Massachusetts in 1783, black freedmen and freedwomen soon learned that freedom came only by degrees. Snide remarks had appeared in the Boston newspapers in the previous year, calling the gathering of black Masons for the traditional Feast of St. John a meeting of "St. Blacks' Lodge of Free and Accepted Masons." And mostly, black Bostonians found only ill-paid work and deep prejudice against them. In 1786, when the Shaysite Rebellion swept Massachusetts, Hall tried to offset white hostility by offering the services of what he called the Commonwealth's "meanest members"—700 blacks of the Boston region—"in this time of trouble and confusion."[19] Acting as spokesman for the large number of free blacks who had flocked to Boston in search of work opportunities, he offered support to the embattled state government in its campaign against agrarian insurgency.

Spurned by the governor and discouraged at their lot, Boston's free black community now turned in an entirely different direction. Hardly six weeks after offering to march against the Shaysites, Prince Hall petitioned the legislature on behalf of the city's African-Americans to support a plan for returning to Africa. Declaring that they lived in "disagreeable and disadvantageous circumstances," which they believed would prevail "so long as we and our children live in America," they wished "earnestly . . . to return to Africa, our native country

... where we shall live among our equals and be more comfortable and happy, than we can be in our present situation. ...."[20] This was one of the first expressions of the black colonization impulse, an early form of black nationalism, that would recur periodically in the North in the following decades. When this plan failed, receiving no assistance from the legislature, Hall continued to organize, protesting the exclusion of black children from tax-supported free schools, protesting against the kidnapping of free blacks into slavery, and calling for the end of the slave trade. He would not cease organizing and protesting in Boston against the "weeds of pride, envy, tyranny, and scorn, in this garden of peace, liberty, and equality" until death removed the pen from his hand and stifled his voice in June 1807, just six months before the slave trade legally expired.[21]

Richard Allen, 24 years younger than Prince Hall, was made of still different clay. In his way of grappling with his identity and with the future of black Americans we can see a different strategy at work. Allen had grown up as a slave to the family of Benjamin Chew, a wealthy, conservative lawyer and proprietary officeholder in Pennsylvania. Sometime in the early 1770s, Chew sold Allen's family to a Delaware farmer. It was here, on the farm of Stokeley Sturgis in Kent County in about 1777, that Allen experienced a religious conversion at the hands of itinerant Methodists, who were criss-crossing the Delaware and Chesapeake peninsulas in this formative period of American Methodism.[22]

Allen's master also fell to the power of the Methodist message, and, nudged along by economic necessity, became enough convinced of the sin of slaveholding to let Allen and his brother purchase their freedom. In 1780, with the war still raging, Allen, age 20, began a six-year religious sojourn, interspersing work as a sawyer, wagon driver, and shoemaker with stints of itinerant preaching that carried him by foot over hundreds of miles, to black and white audiences in dozens of villages, crossroads, and farms. By the mid-1780s, he was well known to the leading Methodist preachers, including Francis Asbury. It was probably through Asbury's intervention that he received the call to go to Philadelphia to preach to the small group of free blacks who were worshiping at St. George's Methodist church, a rude, dirt-floored building in the German part of the city.[23]

Having soon fattened the black Methodist flock, Allen, with Absalom Jones, another Philadelphian recently released from slavery, launched the Free African Society of Philadelphia, the first free black mutual aid association in the new nation. This led, in turn, to a desire for an independent black church. Allen's fervent Methodism brought him into conflict with other emerging black leaders who wished for a nondenominational or "union" church, and thus within a few years two black churches took form. In both cases, the guiding idea was that black Americans emerging from slavery required independent black churches because, as the Philadelphia black leaders phrased it, "men are more influenced by their moral equals than by their superiors," and "are more easily governed by persons chosen by themselves for that purpose than by persons who are placed over them by accidental circumstances." This, it was argued, created the "necessity and propriety of separate and exclusive means, and opportunities, of worshiping God, or instructing their youth, and of taking care of their poor" through separate institutions.[24]

The autonomous black churches founded in Philadelphia only a decade after the war had ended were critically important in furthering the social and psychological liberation of recently freed slaves. The desire "to worship God under our own vine and fig tree" was in essence a desire to stand apart from white society, avoiding both the paternalistic benevolence of its racially liberal members and the animosity of its racially intolerant members.[25] It was this distancing that allowed former slaves to strike out on independent courses in other areas of concern. From Allen's Mother Bethel flowed petitions and sermons against slavery and the slave trade, plans for black schools and mutual aid societies, protests against race discrimination in the city of brotherly love, and, on occasion, emigrationist schemes.

Jupiter Hammon, James Forten, Prince Hall, and Richard Allen represent four forms that the quest for place and self-definition could take as African-Americans emerged from the Revolution. Amidst white Americans who were themselves groping to define their identity as a new nation, blacks individually and in groups had to develop a consciousness of self. Were these newly freed people to regard themselves as Africans in America who might best return to the lands of their ancestors? Prince Hall and 71 of his fellow black Bostonians were the first postrevolutionary Americans that we know of to think so. Or were African-Americans simply Americans with dark skins, who, in seeking places as free men and women, had to adapt as quickly as possible to the cultural norms and social institutions of the dominant white society? James Forten of Philadelphia was such a man in the 1780s. Or were African-Americans a people whose future rested on soil where they had toiled most of their lives but whose cultural heritage was distinctly African and whose necessity was to develop separate black institutions? This was the identity grasped by Jupiter Hammon and Richard Allen, though each in a different way.

Partly because so many African males in their teens and twenties had fled to the British during the war, and partly because revolutions generally call forth talent at an unusually young age, the leaders of black society who emerged in the 1780s and 1790s were mostly young men and women in their twenties and thirties. David George, a runaway slave from Virginia, gathered the first black Baptist church among slaves in Silver Creek, South Carolina, at age 31. Harry Hosier, born a slave in North Carolina in about 1750, had emerged by the early 1780s as an itinerating Methodist preacher with remarkable homiletic gifts. Thomas Coke, an early Methodist leader, called him "one of the best preachers in the world," and Benjamin Rush raised the ante, terming him "the greatest orator in America."[26] Richard Allen was only 26 when he began leading black Methodists in Philadelphia, six years after obtaining his freedom. Peter Spencer, born a slave in Kent County, Maryland, was 23 when he led black Methodists out of the white church in Wilmington, Delaware, in 1805, and Thomas Paul emerged as the most important "exhorter" among Boston's blacks in his early twenties. Daniel Coker, born a slave in Frederick County, Maryland, was only 25 when he became the teacher of the black school in Baltimore, but he had already been preaching for two years. His biting abolitionist pamphlet, *A Dialogue between a Virginian and an African Minister*, came off the press in 1805, before his twentieth-sixth birthday. A few leaders were somewhat older. Prince Hall was 35 before he gained his freedom in Boston in 1770 and emerged as the leader of that city's blacks. Peter Williams was also in his thirties when he emerged as the leader of New York City's black Methodists in the 1790s. But the spiritual gifts of most black religious leaders surfaced very early, and in black communities up and down the seaboard, from Boston to Baltimore, it was not unusual at any point between the end of the Revolution and the 1830s to see very young men in leadership roles.

It is also notable about this generation of young black leaders that they were so widely traveled. In an era of primitive transportation and when their slender means usually precluded any form of travel other than on foot, many of them trekked thousands of miles and knew vast stretches of territory in ways that white males their age, tied to farms and artisan shops in particular locales, seldom experienced. Richard Allen sojourned incessantly for six years between North Carolina and New York in his early twenties, making a living as woodcutter, shoemaker, and wagoner while preaching the gospel. Daniel Coker knew the whole region from New York to Baltimore through his Methodist itinerating. Harry Hosier, who often accompanied Bishop Francis Asbury and other Methodist notables, logged thousands of miles and preached in cities, villages, and farms, to whites as well as blacks, over half the settled area of postrevolutionary America. John Gloucester, the 31-year-old Tennessee slave who became the leader of the first black Presbyterian church in Philadelphia in 1807, traveled for years up and down the Atlantic seaboard and across the Atlantic to England to collect money to free his family from slavery. Nero Prince, a successor of Prince Hall as grand master of the Black Masonic Lodge in Boston, traveled all over the world as a mariner and spent a dozen years as a footman at the court of the Russian czar in the early nineteenth century. Later in life Prince returned to Petrograd with his young wife, Nancy Gardner Prince, and there the couple operated a profitable business making childrens' clothes.[27]

Black spiritual leaders such as David George, Lemuel Haynes, John Marrant, and John Chavis were likewise knowledgeable about regions as remote as Nova Scotia and the Cherokee towns of central and western Appalachia. In most of these cases, geographical knowledgeability had begun when, as slaves, they were sold to owners in distant places or had run far away from the place of their enslavement. In most cases, it was conversion to the Methodist or Baptist faith that led them, after securing their freedom, to an itinerant life. In something akin to biblical journeys into the wilderness, they tested their mettle and proved their faith through ceaseless travel. In doing so, they developed a toughness, a resiliency, a cosmopolitanism, an ability to confront rapidly changing circumstances, and skills in dealing with a wide variety of people and temperaments. This occurred much more rarely among poor white citizens of the republic, who were farm-bound and village-bound and had few venues for learning or displaying such talents. Hence, in the postrevolutionary generation, many of the most notable cases of self-made men, of ascent from the lowest rungs of society to positions of responsibility and influence, involved recently freed slaves.

o   o   o

Between the 1780s and 1820s, during the lifespan of the revolutionary generation, black Americans by the thousands wrestled to find an identity, trying to reconcile their consciousness of being African and their consciousness of being American. For the most part, they solved this problem by living a double existence, or maintaining a dialectical relationship between the two parts of their identity, in what W. E. B. Du Bois called "two unreconciled strivings; two warring ideals in one dark body, whose dogged strength alone keeps it from being torn asunder." Du Bois saw "the history of the American Negro as the history of this strife," and though he never followed it back to the postrevolutionary era, his characterization poignantly describes the early period of black freedom.[28]

It was through the creation of "a culture of alternative institutions" that this founding generation of free black Americans was able to maintain its dialectical existence as both Africans and Americans. "By their presence and their persistence," writes Will B. Gravely, they "contradicted the white vision of America and in its place articulated and lived out an image of the country which could accommodate this dialectic."[29] In this creating of a sense of peoplehood, nothing was more important than the construction of autonomous black churches, which became the "biblical embodiment of the cultural and religious transformation of enslaved Africans into free Afro-Americans."[30]

In the early national period, it was the emerging independent black churches, uniformly named *African* churches, that were most vital in giving free blacks, and slaves within reach of their influence, a sense of peoplehood within a white republic that was becoming increasingly hostile to the free black presence. The "coming out" from white churches, as the decision to leave white churches was expressed, involved a painful and sometimes dangerous process of rebirthing. At the heart of this process of being reborn was the psychologically crucial step of rejecting white definitions of black people's place, definitions which, as Vincent Harding puts it, "had nothing to do with the spirit of a living and just God."[31] It was in challenging the right of white churches to govern them in the area of religion, the bulwark of their existence as free people, that free blacks took their most important step toward self-determination in a white republic determined for the most part to give them no self.

Part of the rising feeling against free blacks in the North and upper South was in fact caused by this psychologically vital move toward self-determination. "Their aspirings and little vanities," sneered a white Methodist in Philadelphia, "have been rapidly growing since they got those separate churches. ... Thirty to forty years ago, they were much humbler, more esteemed in their places, and more useful to themselves and others."[32] Daniel Payne, bishop of the African Methodist-Episcopal church in the mid-nineteenth century, wrote on the opposite side of the same coin some years later that the "unpardonable crime" that free blacks had committed in forming independent churches "was that they dared to organize a Church of men, men to think for themselves, men to talk for themselves, men to act for themselves."[33]

Thus arose a great and tragic paradox: as free blacks removed themselves from white paternalist influence by founding and sustaining their own institutions that were dedicated to guiding the religious, moral, and educational lives of their people, white charges about insurmountable black inferiority intensified. The first period of creative institution building by recently freed slaves was tragically accompanied in the early nineteenth century by the demise of enlightened environmentalist theories that stressed nurture over nature and social conditions over heredity in the forming of the human character. The revival of earlier patterns of racist thought that insisted on innate black inferiority occurred precisely during a period of impressive accomplishment among newly freed slaves.[34]

73

Black leaders vigorously answered such charges of inferiority in the early nineteenth century. Far from inferior, they
saw themselves as "the people of God," a "chosen generation,"
a "holy nation," a "peculiar people," to use the phrases of
Daniel Coker of Baltimore, who like so many other black leaders gave biblical sanction to the passage from slavery to freedom
by likening it to the Hebrew exodus from Egypt.[35] In black
Baptist and Methodist churches throughout the North and upper South, black Christians heard the message repeatedly that,
contrary to white belief, God had not made them inferior to
whites. Indeed, they were superior to white Christians who
were mired in the sins of slaveholding and racism and had
trapped themselves in the logical contradiction of trying to
build a republic of slaveholders. In one of the hymns that
echoed through Richard Allen's Mother Bethel church in Philadelphia in the early nineteenth century, black worshipers sang
out:

> What poor despised company
> Of travellers are these
> That's walking yonder narrow way,
> Along that rugged maze?
>
> Why that are of a royal line,
> They're children of a King;
> Heirs of immortal Crown divine,
> And loud for joy they sing.
>
> Why do they then appear so mean,
> And why so much despis'd?
> Because of their rich robes unseen
> The world is not apprized.[36]

It must have been an elevating thought—and certainly it
was a sustaining one—that God's wrath would descend on the
new nation unless its white inhabitants removed the sin of
slavery. Equally sustaining, perhaps, was the notion that while

white Christians regarded their country as the "redeemer nation," it was black Christians, God's chosen people, who would have to do the real redeeming by weaning white America from un-Christian behavior and thus prepare the nation for the coming millennium.[37] The parallel between black and Hebrew freedom struggles not only linked African-Americans psychologically to the African homeland, where the long journey toward redemption had its origins, but offered insights into the superiority of black culture over white culture in the new nation.

In the independence struggles carried out in their black churches, the postrevolutionary generation of free African-Americans also found their way to an understanding that it was they, rather than their white detractors, who best upheld the revolutionary tradition of freedom, equality, and social justice. In Baltimore, Wilmington, Philadelphia, New York, Boston, New Haven, and many smaller towns African-American Methodists refused to worship under the authority of the white Methodist church. Strengthening black resolve was the abandonment by white Methodists in the early nineteenth century of earlier antislavery commitments; their involvement in the colonization movement that aimed to return all free blacks to Africa; and the persistent interference of white Methodists in crucial areas of congregational life—in matters involving control of church property, congregational discipline, access to ordination, and representation in church-wide governing bodies.

Just as their personal emancipations from slavery had involved a psychological rebirth, the collective emancipation of black churches from white ecclesiastical authority signaled a political maturation. Forty years after Richard Allen, Daniel Coker, and others had founded the independent African Methodist Episcopal Church in 1817, the first historian of the church noted that the black independence movement had been indispensably important in disproving the white notion "that the colored man was incapable of self-government and self-support."

The enormous growth and geographical spread of the AME by the 1850s, asserted Bishop Daniel Payne, was "a flat contradiction and triumphant refutation of this slander, so foul in itself and so degrading in its influence."[38]

Equally, the creation of independent black churches gave black religionists a chance to see how they might improve on the undemocratic governance of white churches. When Allen, Coker, and others launched the AME church in 1816, bringing themselves out from under the ecclesiastical jurisdiction of the white Methodist Episcopal church, they made it clear in their first official pronouncements that they had been driven to this by "spiritual despotism." They vowed to take a different course, "remembering, that we are not to Lord it over God's heritage, as greedy dogs, that can never have enough; but with long suffering and bowels of compassion, to bear each other's burdens, and so fulfil the law of Christ. . . ."[39]

By the early nineteenth century, as the question of race agitated white northern minds and began leading to exclusionist policies, free blacks in the North found themselves caught in a cruel bind. Many whites were convinced that Africans were an inherently inferior people and used this to justify keeping them in servitude; yet when they emerged from bondage, they were excluded from schools and crowded out of work roles where they might acquire the training and means to prove their detractors wrong. Richard Allen chided the white community for this as early as 1794: was it reasonable, he asked, "that a superior good conduct is looked for, from our race, by those who stigmatize us as men, whose baseness is incurable and may therefore be held in a state of servitude, that a merciful man would not deem a beast to; yet you try what you can to prevent our rising from a state of barbarism, you represent us to be in." The circularity of the white argument against abolition was apparent. "Will you," asked Allen, "because you have reduced us to the unhappy condition our color is in, plead our incapacity for freedom . . . as a sufficient cause for keeping us under the grievous yoke?"[40]

When it became clear that the new nation was to be defined as a republic for white men only, free blacks of James Forten's type, who earlier had attempted to adapt to white society and live quiet lives by white, middle-class norms, became thoroughly politicized. This moved them closer to proto-black nationalists like Prince Hall, Paul Cuffee, and others who advocated emigration to Africa, Haiti, or Canada. Alternatively, former assimilationists were pushed toward the strategy represented by Richard Allen—the seeking of separate black institutions as bastions from which to combat white hostility while remaining wedded to an American existence.

While struggling to prove themselves in the northern cities, free blacks became, in a peculiar way, the conscience of the nation. It was they, along with a small number of white reformers, who emerged in the early nineteenth century, as Vincent Harding reminds us, as "the foremost proponents of freedom and justice in the nation, demanding of the Constitution more than its slave-holding creators dared to dream, wrestling it toward an integrity that the [Founding] Fathers would not give it."[41] Five years after its ratification, Absalom Jones and Richard Allen reminded white Americans of the ferocious black insurrection in St. Domingue and warned: "If you love your children, if you love your country, if you love the God of love, clear your hands from slaves, burden not your children or country with them."[42] Struggling to define themselves in a new era, African-Americans were simultaneously attempting "to transform the Constitution of the nation into an instrument of justice for all its people."[43]

With this principle guiding him, Absalom Jones carried a petition to Congress through the streets of Philadelphia in 1797 that he had written on behalf of four North Carolina refugees from slavery whose freedom was imperiled because the Fugitive Slave Law passed by Congress in 1793 gave virtual hunting licenses to southern agents intent on seizing free blacks in northern cities. Could they not expect "public justice" from

the national government? When would the government end
the "unconstitutional bondage" which was "a direct violation
of the declared fundamental principles of the Constitution?"[44]
Attempting to redirect the moral compass of the government
back to the sacred texts of the revolutionary era, Jones, with
a hint of irony, addressed the petition "To the President, Senate, and House of representatives of the—most free and enlightened nation in the world!!!" To drive home the point he
compared the "unconstitutional bondage in which multitudes
of our fellows in complexion are held" with the "deplorable
. . . situation of citizens of the United States captured and
enslaved . . . in Algiers." It was James Madison who rose to
assert that a petition from blacks "had no claim on their attention" in Congress. That august body promptly dismissed
the petition.[45]

Boston's blacks likewise kept the fires of antislavery protest
burning. In 1797, Prince Hall condemned slavery in an address
at the African Masonic Lodge, celebrated the black rebellion
in Santo Domingue, and denounced "the daily insults" suffered
by the city's black citizens "in the streets of Boston . . . on
public days of recreation."[46] Two years later, Philadelphia's
free blacks petitioned the government again, and this time it
was the recently politicized James Forten who shepherded the
petition to Congress.[47] Steadfast to the ark and covenant of
the revolutionary credo, he wrote: "Though our faces are black,
yet we are men, and . . . are as anxious to enjoy the birth-right
of the human race as those who [are white]." Philadelphia's
black leaders knew that in framing the Constitution the 55
delegates at Philadelphia had been unwilling to advertise their
abandonment of revolutionary principles by specifying that
slaves had no natural rights and thus had omitted all mention
of the word slave. Now they put this omission to good use.
"In the Constitution, and in the Fugitive bill," wrote Absalom
Jones, who authored the petition, "no mention is made of Black
people or Slaves—therefore if the Bill of Rights, or the dec-

78

laration of Congress [i.e., the Declaration of Independence] are of any validity, we beseech that as we are *men*, we may be admitted to partake of the Liberties and inalienable Rights therein held forth. . . ."[48]

Philadelphia's black residents again petitioned Congress in 1800, calling for an end to the slave trade, a repeal of the Fugitive Slave Act of 1793, and the gradual end of slavery itself. In these and other documents, blacks kept before the nation the contradiction between the principles of freedom and natural rights embodied in the preamble of the Constitution and the "compromising thrust of the main document."[49] In this same year, Gabriel Prosser, a free black in Richmond, Virginia, organized an attempt to overthrow slavery in the capital of the southern state with the largest number of slaves. When the plot was discovered and its perpetrators put on trial, they built their defense on the same contradiction between slavery and republicanism that the white revolutionary leaders, North and South, had spoken of repeatedly in the revolutionary period and that black leaders had kept before the public's notice. "I have nothing more to offer" in my defense, testified one of Prosser's group, "than what General Washington would have had to offer, had he been taken by the British and put to trial by them. I have adventured my life in endeavouring to obtain the liberty of my countrymen, and I am a willing sacrifice in their cause."[50]

With the end of the slave trade in 1807, at a time when white abolitionism was fading rapidly, northern black clergymen who led independent black churches began to use annual New Year's Day celebrations to keep alive the call for slavery's abolition. They repeatedly invoked the elevated phrases of revolutionary ideology, confronting white Americans with the misalignment between their sacred texts and their continued toleration of slavery. God had surely been listening, wrote Peter Williams, Jr., in New York City in 1808, "when the sons of 76 pronounced these United States free and independent;

when the spirit of patriotism, erected a temple sacred to liberty; when the inspired voice of Americans first uttered those noble sentiments, 'we hold these truths to be self-evident, that all men are created equal; that they are endowed by their Creator with certain inalienable rights'. . . ." How long would it be until "the sun of liberty shall beam resplendent on the whole African race . . . ," when "the inherent rights of man" would be restored to "the bleeding African"?[51] From Boston in the same year came another chiding of white Americans who presumed, in defiance of their own revolutionary principles, to exercise authority over blacks "by depriving us of our freedom, as though they had a command from heaven thus to do."[52]

Such addresses, only a few of which have come down to us in published form, nurtured a feeling of collectivity that, as Gravely has said, "depended on an historical consciousness and the sense of belonging to a tradition" of protest and struggle.[53] Frequently the tradition was carried back to the deliverance of the people of Israel from Egyptian bondage. Thus, just as the Passover liturgy kept alive for every Jew his or her links to the historical Hebrew deliverance from slavery, so black Americans were counseled, as Absalom Jones told his Philadelphia parishioners in 1808, to "remember the rock whence we were hewn and the pit whence we were digg'd." "Let the history of the sufferings of our brethren," lectured Jones, "and of their deliverance, descend by this means to our children, to the remotest generations."[54]

Invoking revolutionary principles and telling stories of biblical deliverance thus had a twofold purpose: first, to keep alive the tradition of protest among black Americans; and second, to keep reminding white Americans of the installments on the revolutionary mortgage on which they were defaulting. What can be witnessed in the early nineteenth century is the nourishing of the black spirit of protest and the moral cudgeling of the white community in the midst of a rising hostility in the North to the growing free black communities.

This growing white hostility became shockingly apparent on the very days that the new nation set aside to celebrate its virtues, its accomplishments, and its bedrock values. As early as 1797, Prince Hall deplored the "daily insults we meet with in the streets of Boston, much more on public days of recreation" when "we may truly be said to carry our lives in our hands. . . ." Such treatment, Hall complained, was not even meted out to slaves in the West Indies, where, he had been assured by a gentleman "that a slave, on Sundays or holidays, enjoys himself and friends without molestation."[55] A few years later in Philadelphia, black citizens suffered similarly. For many years it had been customary for all classes and colors to gather in the square facing the State House where the nation's birth certificate had been signed. Amidst toasting and carousing, the city's leaders would harangue the crowd about the blessings of liberty and the prospects of national greatness. But on this occasion, in about 1805, dozens of sullen white citizens turned on the free blacks assembled for the festivities and drove them from the square with a torrent of curses and a storm of rocks.[56]

Within the next few years calls for restrictive legislation began pouring into Pennsylvania's legislature—calls for limiting the entry of free blacks into the state, for passing special taxes on blacks for the support of their poor, for requiring free blacks to carry registration certificates. Legislators drew up bills to cordon off Pennsylvania and circumscribe the rights of those free blacks already there.

Black Pennsylvanians could not stem the tide of this white racial hostility. But, at a time when the white abolitionist impulse was fading, they could continue to build the sustaining connective tissue of their own communities, and they could keep alive a tradition of protest by holding up the principles of 1776 and 1787 before white petitioners and legislators in order to show them how far they had strayed from their own faith. "We hold this truth to be self-evident," wrote James Forten in *Letters by A Man of Color* (1813), "that God created all men equal, is one of the most prominent features in the Declaration of Independence, and in that glorious fabric of collected wisdom, our noble Constitution. This idea embraces the Indian and the European, the savage and the Saint, the Peruvian and the Laplander, the white man and the African, and whatever measures are adopted subversive of this inestimable privilege, are in direct violation of the letter and spirit of our Constitution. . . ."[57]

Forten also invoked the Pennsylvania constitution of 1790 to show white leaders how faithless they were to their own credo. The patriotic citizens of Pennsylvania, he reminded them, passed a constitution "for the protection of those inestimable rights" that included the declaration that "All men are born equally free and independent, and have certain inherent and indefeasible rights, among which are those of enjoying [and defending] life and liberty." The legislators who had drawn up restrictive legislation, charged Forten, apparently "mistook the sentiment expressed in this article, and do not consider us as men." "Has the God who made the white man and the black left any record declaring us a different species? Are we not sustained by the same power, supported by the same food, hurt by the same wounds, wounded by the same wrongs, pleased with the same delights, and propagated by the same means?" Forten dispatched the white legislators back to the revolutionary generation. "It cannot be that the authors of our Constitution intended to exclude us from its benefits, for just emerging from unjust and cruel emancipation, their souls were too much affected with their own deprivations to commence the reign of terror over others. They knew we were deeper skinned than they were, but they acknowledged us as men, and found that many an honest heart beat beneath a dusky bosom. They felt that they had no more authority to enslave us, than England had to tyrannize over them." Thus, they declared " 'all men' free, [and] did not particularize white and black, because they never supposed it would be made a question whether *we were men or not*. Sacred be the ashes, and deathless be the memory of those heroes who are dead."⁵⁸

Thus did free black Americans in the North in the early nineteenth century attempt to hold the postrevolutionary generation to its founding principles. The grand irony of the era of early nationhood is, as Vincent Harding puts it, "the children of Africa, whose freedom the Constitution makers sacrificed on the altar of a tenuous and limited white unity," were the Americans who "pressed the nation toward its highest possibilities" and toward a more perfect union.⁵⁹

NOTES

1. The mid-nineteenth-century black historian William C. Nell was the first to give attention to the subject, but his *Colored Patriots of the American Revolution* (Boston, 1855) was written during the height of the antislavery crusade and was meant to win favor by showing that blacks had fought valiantly in the struggle for independence. It thus ignored the much larger number of slaves who fought with the British as a way of gaining their personal liberty. The first modern treatment, and still the most comprehensive, is Benjamin Quarles, *The Negro in the American Revolution* (Chapel Hill, N. C., 1961). Other worthy studies are Jeffrey J. Crow, *The Black Experience in Revolutionary North Carolina* (Raleigh, N. C., 1977); Peter H. Wood, " 'Taking Care of Business' in Revolutionary South Carolina: Republicanism and the Slave Society," in Jeffrey J. Crow and Larry E. Tise, eds., *The Southern Experience in the American Revolution* (Chapel Hill, N. C., 1978); and Wood, " 'Impatient of Oppression': Black Freedom Struggles on the Eve of White Independence," *Southern Exposure*, 12, no. 6 (1984), 10–16.

2. Quoted in Wood, " 'Impatient of Oppression,' " 10.

3. *The Appendix: or, some Observations on the expediency of the Petition of the Africans, living in Boston* ... (Boston, [1773]), 9–11.

4. "The Petition of the Negroes in the Towns of Stratford and Fairfield in the County of Fairfield who are held in a State of Slavery,"

in Herbert Aptheker, ed., *A Documentary History of the Negro People in the United States* (2 vols.; New York, 1951), I, 7–8, 10–12. (See Documents, p. 175.)

5. *The Journals of Henry Melchior Muhlenberg*, trans. Theodore G. Tappert and John W. Doberstein (3 vols.; Philadelphia, 1942–58), III, 78.

6. Quoted in William Nelson, *The American Tory* (New York, 1961), 111–12.

7. Thomas Jefferson to William Gordon, July 16, 1788, in Julian P. Boyd et al., eds., *The Papers of Thomas Jefferson* (Princeton, N. J., 1950–), XIII, 364.

8. Contemporaries estimated a loss of one-quarter of some 100,000 South Carolina slaves during the war; if adult males made up one-third of the population and if most of the losses were of adult males, then the proportion of able-bodied males who fled may have been even higher. For estimates of loss of slaves see Robert M. Weir, "South Carolina: Slavery and the Structure of the Union," in Michael Allen Gillespie and Michael Lienesch, eds., *Ratifying the Constitution* (Lawrence, Kan., 1989), 202.

9. *Pennsylvania Packet*, Dec. 12, 1779.

10. Graham R. Hodges, *African-Americans in Monmouth County During the Age of the American Revolution* (Lincroft, N. J., 1990), 13–23.

11. Phillip M. Richards, "Nationalist Themes in the Preaching of Jupiter Hammon," *Early American Literature*, forthcoming.

12. Richards, "Nationalist Themes"; Jupiter Hammon, "A Winter's Piece," in *America's First Negro Poet: The Complete Works of Jupiter Hammon of Long Island*, ed. Stanley Austin Ransom (Port Washington, N. Y., 1970), 67–85.

13. "An Address to the Negroes," in *Works of Hammon*, 106–18.

14. Ibid., 107.

15. Nell, *Colored Patriots of the American Revolution*, 167–70.

16. For Forten's role as a leader in Philadelphia, see Gary B. Nash, *Forging Freedom: The Making of Philadelphia's Black Community, 1720–1840* (Cambridge, Mass., 1988), passim; and Julie Winch, *Philadelphia's Black Elite: Activism, Accommodation, and the Struggle for Autonomy, 1787–1848* (Philadelphia, 1988), passim.

17. Quoted in Sidney Kaplan, *The Black Presence in the Era of the American Revolution, 1770–1800* (Greenwich, Conn., 1973), 11–13.

18. Quoted in ibid., 184.

19. Quoted in ibid., 184.

20. Quoted in ibid., 186.

21. Quoted in ibid., 187–92.

22. Gary B. Nash, "New Light on Richard Allen: The Early Years," *William and Mary Quarterly*, 3rd ser., 46 (1989), 332–40.

23. Nash, *Forging Freedom*, 95–98.

24. "Address of Representatives of the African Church," in *Extract of a Letter from Dr. Benjamin Rush, of Philadelphia, to Granville Sharp* (London, 1792), 6–7.

25. Richard Allen, *The Life Experience and Gospel Labors of Rt. Rev. Richard Allen* . . . (Nashville, Tenn., 1960), 26.

26. Lewis V. Baldwin, *Invisible Strands in African Methodism: A History of the African Union Methodist Protestant and Union African Methodist Episcopal Churches, 1805–1980* (Philadelphia, 1983), 24.

27. *Autobiography of Nancy Gardner* (1850), cited in Dorothy Sterling, *We Are Your Sisters: Black Women in the Nineteenth Century* (New York, 1984), 94–95.

28. W. E. Burghardt Du Bois, *The Souls of Black Folk* (New York, 1970), 3.

29. William B. Gravely, "The Dialectic of Double-Consciousness in Black American Freedom Celebrations, 1808–1863," *Journal of Negro History*, 67 (1982), 302.

30. Will B. Gravely, "The Rise of African Churches in America (1786–1822): Re-examining the Contexts," *Journal of Religious Thought*, 41 (1984), 58.

31. Vincent Harding, *There is a River: The Black Struggle for Freedom in America* (New York, 1981), 44.

32. John F. Watson, *Annals of Philadelphia* . . . (3 vols.; Philadelphia, 1830; reprint 1900), II, 261.

33. Daniel Payne, *History of the African Methodist Episcopal Church* (1891; reprint, New York, 1969), 9–10.

34. The withering of environmentalist thinking on race is traced in George M. Frederickson, *The Black Image in the White Mind: The Debate on Afro-American Character and Destiny, 1817–1914* (New York,

1971); and Larry E. Tise, *Proslavery: A History of the Defense of Slavery in America, 1701–1840* (Athens, Ga., 1987).

35. The phrases are in Daniel Coker's *A Dialogue between a Virginian and an African Minister* (Baltimore, 1810); and *A Sermon, delivered extempore in the African Episcopal Church in the city of Baltimore . . .* ([Baltimore, 1816]).

36. Richard Allen, *A Collection of Hymns and Spiritual Songs From Various Authors* (Philadelphia, 1801), 17.

37. Albert J. Raboteau, "The Black Experience in American Evangelicalism: The Meaning of Slavery," in Leonard I. Sweet, ed., *The Evangelical Tradition in America* (Macon, Ga., 1984), 181–97.

38. Payne, *History of the African Methodist Episcopal Church*, 10.

39. Richard Allen, Daniel Coker, and James Champion, *The Doctrines and Discipline of the African Methodist Episcopal Church* (Philadelphia, 1817), 9

40. A[bsalom] J[ones] and R[ichard] A[llen], *A Narrative of the Proceedings of the Black People, During the Late Awful Calamity in Philadelphia, in the year 1793 . . .* (Philadelphia, 1794), 23–24. (See Documents, p. 184.)

41. Vincent Harding, "Wrestling toward the Dawn: The Afro-American Freedom Movement and the Changing Constitution," *Journal of American History*, 74 (1987), 719.

42. Jones and Allen, *Narrative of the Proceedings*, 22. (See Documents, pp. 182–84.)

43. Harding, "Wrestling toward the Dawn," 720.

44. The petition is reprinted in Aptheker, *Documentary History*, 40–44. (See Documents, p. 189.)

45. Donald L. Robinson, *Slavery in the Structure of American Politics, 1765–1820* (New York, 1971), 287–90.

46. Quoted in James and Lois Horton, *Black Bostonians: Family Life and Community Struggle in the Antebellum North* (New York, 1979), 29–30.

47. The petition is printed in John Parrish, *Remarks on the Slavery of the Black People . . .* (Philadelphia, 1806), 51–52.

48. Petition of the free blacks of Philadelphia to the President and Congress of the United States, Dec. 31, 1799, excerpted in Kaplan, *Black Presence*, 237–39.

49. Harding, "Wrestling toward the Dawn," 721.

50. Robert Sutcliff, *Travels in Some Parts of North America, in the Years 1804, 1805, & 1806* (York, Eng., 1815), quoted in Leon Litwack, "Trouble in Mind: The Bicentennial and the Afro-American Experience," *Journal of American History*, 74 (1987), 318.

51. Peter Williams, Jr., *An Oration on the Abolition of the Slave Trade* ... (New York, 1808), excerpted in Aptheker, *Documentary History*, 51.

52. *The Sons of Africa: An Essay on Freedom* ... (Boston, 1808), excerpted in Aptheker, *Documentary History*, 52.

53. Gravely, "The Dialectic of Double-Consciousness," 307.

54. Absalom Jones, *A Thanksgiving Sermon Preached January 1, 1808 ... on Account of the Abolition of the African Slave Trade* (Philadelphia, 1808), 17, 19.

55. Prince Hall, "A Charge Delivered to the African Lodge, June 24, 1797, at Menotomy, Massachusetts," in Benjamin G. Brawley, *Early Negro Writers* (Chapel Hill, N. C., 1935), 98–99.

56. James Forten, *A Series of Letters by A Man of Colour* (Philadelphia, 1813). (See Documents, p. 196.)

57. Ibid. (See Documents, p. 190.)

58. Ibid. (See Documents, pp. 192–93.)

59. Harding, "Wrestling toward the Dawn," 719.

A
SERIOUS ADDRESS

TO THE

RULERS of AMERICA,

On the Inconfiftency of their Conduct refpecting

SLAVERY:

FORMING A CONTRAST

Between the ENCROACHMENTS of England on
American LIBERTY,

AND,

American INJUSTICE in tolerating SLAVERY.

---

*As for me, I will affuredly contend for full and impartial
liberty, whether my labour may be fuccefsful or vain.*

TRENTON:

Printed by ISAAC COLLINS,

M.DCC.LXXXIII.

The first page of David Cooper's pamphlet "A Serious Address to the Rulers of America, On the Inconsistency of their Conduct respecting Slavery . . ." Page 117. *The Library Company of Philadelphia.*

DOCUMENTS

Documents for Chapter 1

THE REVOLUTIONARY GENERATION
EMBRACES ABOLITIONISM

1. Arthur Lee, "Address on Slavery," Rind's
   Virginia Gazette, March 19, 1767

Son of an aristocratic, slave-owning Virginia family, Arthur Lee studied medicine at the University of Edinburgh and wrote this attack on slavery shortly after returning to Virginia. Fearful of the growing slave population and its effects on the white population, and infected by the antislavery ideas beginning to blossom on both sides of the Atlantic, he was attempting to persuade the Virginia House of Burgesses to prohibit further importation of slaves from Africa. So great was the protest to this essay, that the publisher of the *Virginia Gazette* would not publish its sequel. But Lee had the satisfaction of seeing the Virginia legislature pass a higher import duty on slaves shortly after this essay appeared. This was some discouragement to the slave trade (which the Continental Congress would halt seven years later).

To Mr. Rind,

Sir— Permit me, in your paper, to address the members of our Assembly, on two points, in which the publick interest is very dearly concern'd.

The abolition of Slavery & the Retrieval of Specie, in this Colony, are the Subjects, on which I would bespeak their Attention. They are both to be accomplish'd by the same means.

Chosen as you are, Gentlemen, to watch over & provide for the publick weal and Welfare, whatever is offer'd, as tending to those desirable purposes, will I hope, meet from you a favourable ear. And, be the fate of my Sentiments as it will, I flatter myself that your pardon at least will be Indulged to the Writer.

Long and serious Reflection upon the nature & Consequences of Slavery, has Convinced me, that it is a Violation both of Justice and Religion; that it is dangerous to the safety of the Community in which it prevails; that it is destructive to the growth of arts & Sciences; and lastly, that it produces a numerous & very fatal train of Vices, both in the Slave, and in his Master. To prove these assertions, shall be the purpose of the following essay.

That Slavery, then, is a violation of Justice, will plainly appear when we consider what Justice is. It is simply & truly defin'd, as by Justinian, constans et perpetua voluntas jus suum cuique tribuendi, a constant Endeavour to give every man his right.

Now, as freedom is unquestionably the birth-right of all mankind, of Africans as well as Europeans, to keep the former in a State of slavery is a constant violation of that right, and therefore of Justice.

The ground on which the civillians, who favour Slavery, admit it to be just, Namely, Consent, force, and birth, is totally disputable. For surely a Man's own will or Consent, cannot be allow'd to introduce so important an innovation into society as that of Slavery, or to make himself an out-law, which is really the State of a Slave, since neither Consenting to nor aiding the Laws of ye Society, in which he lives, he is neither bound to obey them, nor entitled to their protection. To found any right in force, is to frustrate all right, and involve every thing in confusion, violence and rapine. With these two the last must fall, since if the Parent cannot be justly made a Slave, neither can the Child be born in Slavery. Le droit des gens, a voulu que les prisoniers, &c.

"The law of nations," says Baron Montesquieu, "has doom'd pris-
oners to Slavery, to prevent their being Slain. The Roman civil law,
permitted debtors whom their Creditors might treat ill, to Sell themselves. And the Law of nature requires that children, whom their
parents, being Slaves, cannot maintain, should be slaves like them.
These reasons of the Civillians are not just; it is not true that a
Captive may be slain, unless in case of absolute necessity; but if he
hath been reduced to slavery it is plain that no such necessity existed,
since he was not slain.

It is not true that a freeman can sell himself. For sale supposes
a price, but in this act the Slave & his property becomes immediately
that of his Master, the slave therefore can receive no price, nor the
Master pay &c. And if a man cannot sell himself, nor a prisoner of
war be reduced to Slavery, much less can his Child." Such are the
Sentiments of this illustrious civillian; his reasonings, which I have
been obliged to contract, the reader, interested in this subject, will
do well to consult at large.

Yet even these rights of impossition very questionable, nay, re-
futable as they are, we have not to authorize the Bondage of the
Africans. For neither do they consent to be our Slaves, nor do we
purchase them of their Conquerors. The British Merchants obtain
them from Africa by violence, artifice & treachery, with a few trinkets
to prompt those unfortunate & destestable people to enslave one
another by force or Strategem. Purchase them indeed they may, under
the authority of an act of British Parliment. An act entailing upon
the Africans, with whom we were not at war, and over whom a
British Parliment could not of right assume even a shadow of authority, the dreadfull curse of perpetual slavery upon them and their
children forever. There cannot be in nature, there is not in all history,
an instance in which every right of men is more flagrantly violated.
The laws of the Antients never authorized the making slaves but of
those nations whom they had conquer'd; yet they were Heathens and
we are Christians. They were misled by a false and monstrous religion, divested of humanity, by a horrible & Barbarous worship; we
are directed by the unering preceps of the revealed religion we possess, enlightened by its wisdom, and humanized by its benevolence.
Before them were gods deformed with passions, and horrible for
every cruelty & Vice; before us is that incomparable pattern of Meek-

ness, Charity, love, and justice to mankind, which so transcendently distinguished the founder of Christianity and his ever amiable doctrines. Reader—remember that the corner stone of your religion is to do unto others as you wou'd they shou'd do unto you; ask then your own Heart, whether it would not abhor anyone, as the most outrageous violator of this & every other principle of right, Justice & humanity, who should make a slave of you and your Posterity forever. Remember that God knoweth the heart. Lay not this flattering unction to your Soul, that it is the custom of the Country, that you found it so, that not your will, but your Necessity consents; Ah think, how little such an excuse will avail you in that awfull day, when your Saviour shall pronounce judgment upon you for breaking a law too plain to be misunderstood, too sacred to be violated. If we say that we are Christians, yet act more inhumanly and unjustly than Heathens, with what dreadfull justice must this Sentence of our blessed Saviours fall upon us: Not every one that sayeth unto me, Lord, Lord, shall enter into the Kingdom of Heaven; but he that doeth the will of my Father which is in heaven. Think a moment how much your temporal, your eternal wellfare, depends upon the abolition of a practice, which deforms the Image of your God; tramples on his reveal'd will, infringes the most Sacred rights, and violates humanity.

Enough I hope has been said to prove that slavery is in violation of justice and religion. That it is dangerous to the safety of the State in which it prevails, may be as safely asserted.

What one's own experience hath not taught, that of others must decide. From hence does history derive its utility. For being, when truly written, a faithfull record of the transactions of mankind, and the consequences that flow'd from them; we are thence furnished with the means of judging what will be the probable effect of transactions similar amoung ourselves. We learn then from history, that slavery, wherever encouraged, has sooner or later been productive of very dangerous commotions. I will not trouble my reader here with quotations in support of this assertion, but content myself with referring those, who may be dubious of its truth, to the histories of Athens, Lacedaemon, Rome, and Spain. And that this observation may bear its full weight, let me beg that it be remember'd these states were remarkable for being the most warlike in the world; the bravest and best trained to discipline and arms.

That we are not such is but too obvious. Yet it does not appear that the slaves in those Communitys, were so numerous as they are in ours. Demothenes during his orphanage, had been defrauded of a large fortune; and in his oration for retrieving it enumerates 52 Slaves. Tacitus, in mentioning a roman Nobleman, who was assassinated by one of his Slaves; records the whole number amounting to 400, to have suffered Death for that crime. From these facts we may conclude, that the proportion of slaves among the antients was not so great as with us; and as, notwithstanding this, the freemen, tho' infinitely better armed and disciplined than we are, were yet brought to the very brink of ruin by the insurrections of their Slaves; what powerfull reasons have not we, to fear even more fatal consequences from the greater prevalence of Slavery among us. How long how bloody and destructive, was the contest between the Moorish slaves and the native Spaniards, and after almost deluges of blood had been shed, the Spaniards obtain'd nothing more, than driving them into the mountains; from whence they remain themselves subjected to their perpetual inroads. Less bloody indeed, though not less alarming, have been the insurrections in Jamaica; and to imagine that we shall be forever exempted from this Calamity, which experience teaches us to be inseperable from slavery, so encouraged, is an infatuation as astonishing, as it will be surely fatal. On us, or on our posterity, the inevitable blow, must, one day, fall; and probably with the most irresistable vengeance the longer it is protracted. Since time, as it adds strength and experience to the slaves, will sink us into perfect security and indolence, which debillitating our minds, and enervating our bodies, will render us an easy conquest to the feeblest foe. Un-arm'd already and undisciplined, with our Militia laws contemned, neglected or perverted, we are like the wretch at the feast; with a drawn sword depending over his head by a Single hair; yet we flatter ourselves, in opposition to the force of reason and conviction of experience, that the danger is not imminent.

To prosecute this Subject farther, at present, would I perceive Mr. Rind, engross too much of your paper, and most likely disgust the reader, I must therefore take leave to defer what remains to the next week. Happy shall I be if my poor attempts should prompt more able Heads to think and write upon a Subject, of such lasting import to the welfare of the Community. Strongly, I confess, am I attached to the positions here laid down, because they are formed upon long and serious deliberation; Yet I am open to that conviction, which truth ever operates on minds unseduced by Interest, and uninflamed by passion.

I am, Sir,
Your humble Servant

Philanthropos

2. Anthony Benezet, *A Caution and Warning to Great-Britain and Her Colonies, in a Short Representation of the Calamitous State of the Enslaved Negroes in the British Dominions . . .* (Philadelphia, 1767)

Members of the Society of Friends (Quakers) had been in the vanguard of the small antislavery movement in America since the 1680s, although it was not until the 1750s that the Society at large began to take action against slaveholding among its own members. Anthony Benezet, son of a Huguenot immigrant to Pennsylvania, was the most tireless of the outspoken Quakers who argued against slavery in the revolutionary era. He was also the most strenuous opponent of the idea of innate African inferiority—a notion widely subscribed to by white American colonists. As a teacher of young children, both black and white, he reached the conclusion that no innate differences in learning capacity existed between them. This fragment of Benezet's long pamphlet set the tone for much of the debate over slavery during the revolutionary period by connecting the cause of American rights with the rights of Africans in America. With this pamphlet, reprinted in London and translated into French, Benezet became an international figure in the early struggle against slavery.

At a Time when the general Rights and Liberties of Mankind, and the Preservation of those valuable Privileges, transmitted to us from our Ancestors, are become so much the Subjects of universal Consideration; can it be an Enquiry indifferent to any, how many of those who distinguish themselves as the Advocates of Liberty, remain insensible and inattentive to the Treatment of Thousands and Tens of Thousands of our Fellow-Men, who, from Motives of Avarice, and the inexorable Decree of Tyrant Custom, are at this very Time kept in the most deplorable State of Slavery, in many Parts of the *British* Dominions?

The Intent of publishing the following Sheets, is more fully to make known the aggravated Iniquity attending the Practice of the Slave-trade; whereby many Thousands of our Fellow-Creatures, as free as ourselves by Nature, and equally with us the Subjects of Christ's redeeming Grace, are yearly brought into inextricable and barbarous Bondage; and many, very many, to miserable and untimely Ends.

The Truth of this lamentable Complaint is so obvious to Persons of Candour, under whose Notice it hath fallen, that several have lately published their Sentiments thereon, as a Matter which calls for the most serious Consideration of all who are concerned for the civil or religious Welfare of their Country. How an Evil, of so deep a Dye, hath so long not only passed uninterrupted by Those in Power, but hath even had their Countenance, is indeed surprising, and, Charity would suppose, must, in a great Measure, have arisen from this, that many Persons in Government, both of the Clergy and Laity, in whose Power it hath been to put a Stop to the Trade, have been unacquainted with the corrupt Motives which give Life to it; and the Groans, the dying Groans, which daily ascend to God, the common Father of Mankind, from the broken Hearts of those his deeply oppressed Creatures; otherwise the Powers of the Earth would not, I think I may venture to say, could not, have so long authorised a Practice so inconsistent with every Idea of Liberty and Justice, which, as the learned *James Foster says, Bids that God, which is the God and Father of the Gentiles, unconverted to Christianity, most daring and bold Defiance; and spurns at all the Principles both of natural and revealed Religion.*

Much might justly be said of the temporal Evils which attend this Practice, as it is destructive of the Welfare of human Society, and of the Peace and Prosperity of every Country, in Proportion as it prevails. It might be also shewn, that it destroys the Bonds of natural Affection and Interest, whereby Mankind in general are united; that it introduces Idleness, discourages Marriage, corrupts the Youth, ruins and debauches Morals, excites continual Apprehensions of Dangers, and frequent Alarms, to which the Whites are necessarily exposed from so great an Encrease of a People, that, by their Bondage and Oppressions, become natural Enemies, yet, at the same time, are filling the Places, and eating the Bread of those who would be the Support and Security of the Country. But as these, and many more Reflections of the same Kind, may occur to a considerate Mind, I shall only endeavour to shew, from the Nature of the Trade, the Plenty which *Guiney* affords its Inhabitants, the barbarous Treatment of the *Negroes*, and the Observations made thereon by Authors of Note, that it is inconsistent with the plainest Precepts of the Gospel, the Dictates of Reason, and every common Sentiment of Humanity. . . .

3. Samuel Hopkins, *A Dialogue Concerning the Slavery of the Africans; Shewing it to be the* Duty *and* Interest *of the* American *Colonies to emancipate all their* African *Slaves* ... (Norwich, Conn., 1776)

Samuel Hopkins was an evangelical Congregationalist minister who lived in a region where slaves were not nearly so numerous as in the South but where the American slave trade was headquartered. By the mid-1700s, his town of Newport, Rhode Island, had become a center of the slave trade. Hopkins was appalled at the auctioning of slaves almost in the shadow of his church. Believing deeply in the concept of divine rewards and punishments, he became convinced that stopping the slave trade in 1774 had earned the rebelling American colonies God's pleasure. But he was equally certain that the country risked God's wrath if it did not end slavery altogether. In this pamphlet, circulated to all the members of the Second Continental Congress in 1776, Hopkins issued one of the first and most unequivocal calls for the emancipation of all slaves. His double appeal—both to morality and self-interest—set the pattern for many later pamphlets. The dialogue form of his argument also tells us much about the arguments of those who defended slavery.

To The Honorable Members of the Continental Congress, Representatives of the THIRTEEN UNITED AMERICAN COLONIES.

MUCH HONORED GENTLEMEN, As God, the great father of the universe, has made you the fathers of these Colonies, and in answer to the prayers of his people given you counsel, and that wisdom and integrity, in the exertion of which you have been such great and extensive blessings and obtained the approbation and applause of your constituents and the respect and veneration of the nations in whose sight you have acted in the important, noble struggle for LIBERTY: We naturally look to you in behalf of more than half a million of persons in these Colonies, who are under such a degree of oppression and tyranny, as to be wholly deprived of all civil and personal liberty, to which they have as good a right as any of their fellow men, and are reduced to the most abject state of bondage and slavery, without any just cause.

We have particular encouragement thus to apply to you, since you have had the honor and happiness of leading these Colonies to resolve to stop the slave trade, and to buy no more slaves imported from Africa. We have the satisfaction of the best assurances that you have done this not merely from political reasons; but from a conviction of the unrighteousness and cruelty of that trade and a regard to justice and benevolence, deeply sensible of the inconsistence of promoting the slavery of the Africans, at the same time we are asserting our own civil liberty, at the risque of our fortunes and lives. This leaves in our minds no doubt of your being sensible of the equal unrighteousness and oppression, as well as inconsistence with our selves, in holding of so many hundreds of thousands of blacks in slavery, who have an equal right to freedom with ourselves, while we are maintaining this struggle for our own and our children's liberty: and a hope and confidence that the cries and tears of these oppressed will be regarded by you; and that your wisdom and the great influence you have in these colonies, will be so properly and effectually exerted, as to bring about a total abolition of slavery, in such a manner as shall greatly promote the happiness of those oppressed strangers, and [the] best interest of the public.

There are many difficulties and obstacles, we are sensible, in the way of this good work: but when the propriety, importance, and necessity of it, come into view, we think ourselves warranted to address you, in the words spoken to Ezra, on an occasion not wholly dissimilar. 'Arise: for this matter belongeth unto you; we also will be with you: be of good courage and do it.'

The righteous and merciful governor of the world has given the greatest encouragement to go on and thoroughly execute judgment, and deliver the spoiled out of the hand of the oppressor, both in his

word, and in the wonderful things he has done for us since we have
began to reform this public iniquity. But if we stop here, what will
be the consequence!

It is observable, that when the Swiss were engaged in their struggle for liberty, in which they were so remarkably succeeded, they
entered into the following public resolve. "No Swiss shall take away
any thing by violence from another, neither in time of war, nor
peace."* How reasonable and important is it that we should at this
time heartily enter into, and thoroughly execute such a resolution!
And that this implies the emancipation of all our African slaves surely
none can doubt.

In this view, the following dialogue is humbly offered to your
perusal, hoping that it may have your approbation and patronage.

May you judge the poor of the people save the children of the
needy, relieve the oppressed, and deliver the spoiled out of the hand
of the oppressor; and be the happy instruments of procuring and
establishing universal LIBERTY to white and black, to be transmitted
down to the latest posterity!

With high esteem, and the most friendly sentiments, We are,
honorable Gentlemen, your very humble servants,

The EDITORS.

A DIALOGUE, &c.

A. Sir, What do you think of the motion made by some among
us, to free all our *African* slaves?—They say, that our holding these
blacks in slavery, as we do, is an open violation of the law of God,
and is so great an instance of unrighteousness and cruelty, that we
cannot expect deliverance from present calamities, and success in
our struggle for liberty in the *American* colonies, until we repent,
and make all the restitution in our power. For my part, I think they
carry things much too far on this head; and if any thing might be
done for the freedom of our slaves, this is not a proper time to attend
to it, while we are in such a state of war and distress, and public
affairs of much greater importance demand all our attention, and the
utmost exertion of the public.

*Dr. ZUBLY's Short Account, p. 41.

B. Sir, I am glad you have introduced this subject, especially, as
you own a number of these slaves; I shall attend to it with pleasure,
and offer my sentiments upon it freely, expecting you will as freely
propose the objections you shall have against any thing I shall advance.
And I take leave here to observe, that if the slavery in which we hold
the blacks, is wrong; it is a very great and public sin; and therefore
a sin which God is now testifying against in the calamities he has
brought upon us, consequently must be reformed, before we can
reasonably expect deliverance, or even sincerely ask for it. It would
be worse than madness then, to put off attention to this matter under
the notion of attending to more important affairs. This is acting like
the mariner, who, when his leaky ship is filling with water, neglects
to stop the leak, or ply the pump, that he may mend his sails. There
are at the lowest computation, 800,000 slaves in *British America*,
including the *West-India* islands; and above half a million of these
are in the colonies on the continent. And if this is in every instance
wrong, unrighteousness and oppression; it must be a very great and
crying sin, there being nothing of the kind equal to it on the face of
the earth. There are but few of these slaves indeed in *New-England*,
compared with the vast numbers in the islands & the southern colonies; and they are treated much better on the continent, and especially among us, than they are in the *West-Indies*. But if it be all
wrong, and real oppression of the poor helpless blacks, we, by refusing to break this yoke, and let these injured captives go free, do
practically justify and support this slavery in general, and make ourselves, in a measure at least, answerable for the whole: and we have
no way to exculpate ourselves from the guilt of the whole, and bear
proper testimony against this great evil, but by freeing all our slaves.
Surely then this matter admits of no delay, but demands our first, and
most serious attention, and speedy reformation.

A. I acknowledge the *slave trade*, as it has been carried on with
the Africans, cannot be justified. But I am not yet convinced that 'tis
wrong to keep those in perpetual bondage, who by this trade have
been transported from *Africa* to us, and are become our slaves. If I
viewed this in the light you do, I should agree with you that 'tis of
the highest importance that they should all be made free without
delay; as we could not expect the favor of heaven, or with any consistency ask it, so long as they are held in bondage.

B. I am glad you have attended to the affair so much as to be convinced of the unrighteousness of the slave trade. Indeed, this conviction has been so spread of late, that it has reached almost all men on the continent, except some of those who are too deeply interested in it to admit the light, which condemns it. And it has now but few advocates, I believe, being generally condemned and exploded. And the members of the continental congress have done themselves much honor, in advising the *American* colonies to drop this trade entirely; and resolving not to buy another slave, that shall be imported from *Africa*.

But I think it of importance that this trade should not only be condemned as wrong, but attentively considered in its real nature, and in all its shocking attendants and circumstances, which will lead us to think of it with a detestation and horror which this scene of inhumanity, oppression, and cruelty, exceeding every thing of the kind that has ever been perpetrated by the sons of men, is suited to excite; and awaken us to a proper indignation against the authors of this violence and outrage done to their fellow men; and to feelings of humanity and pity towards our brethren, who are the miserable sufferers. Therefore, tho' I am not able to paint this horrid scene of barbarity and complicated iniquity, to the life, or even to tell the one half which may be told, in the short time alotted for this conversation; yet I will suggest a few particulars; leaving you, if you please, to consult the authors who have given a more particular description.

Most of the *Africans* are in a state of heathenism; and sunk down into that ignorance and barbarity, into which mankind naturally fall, when destitute of divine revelation. Their lands are fertile, and pro-duce all the necessaries of life, the inhabitants are divided into many distinct nations or clans; and of course are frequently entering into quarrels, and open war with each other. The *Europeans, English, French, Dutch,* &c. have carried on a trade with them for above 100 years; and have taken advantage of their ignorance and barbarity, to perswade them to enter into the inhuman practice of selling one another to the *Europeans*, for the commodities which they carry to them, most of which, they stand in no real need of: but might live as well, or better without them: particularly spirituous liquors, which have been carried to them in great quantities, by the *Americans*. They by this means have tempted and excited the poor blacks to make war upon one another, in order to get captives, spreading distress, devastation and destruction over a vast country; by which many millions have perished: and millions of others, have been captivated, and sold to the *Europeans* & *Americans*, into a state of slavery, much worse than death. And the inhabitants of the towns near the sea, are taught to exert all the art and power they have to entrap and decoy one another, that they may make slaves of them, and sell them to us for rum, by which they intoxicate them selves, and become more brutish and savage than otherwise they could be, so that there are but few instances of sobriety, honesty, or even humanity, in these towns on the sea, to which the *Europeans* have access: and they who live the furthest from these places, are the least vicious, and much more civil and humane.

They stand in no need of the rum that is carried there in such vast quantities, by which so many thousands have been enslaved, and which has spread such infinite mischief among them. And I leave it with you to consider to what a dreadful degree the *Americans* have by this abominable practice, bro't the curse upon them, pronounced by an inspired prophet; and how very applicable it is to this case. "Woe unto him that giveth his neighbour drink: that puttest thy bottle to him, and makest him drunken also, that thou mayst look on their nakedness."* And is not this curse evidently come upon us, in a dreadful degree, in such a way, as to paint itself out, so that he who runs may read it? We have put the bottle to our neighbours mouths, by carrying immense quantities of rum to them, and inticed them to drink, that we might take advantage of their weakness, and thereby gratify our lusts. By this means multitudes of them have been enslaved, and carried to the *West-India* islands, there to be kept to hard labour, and treated ten thousand times worse than dogs. In consequence of which, incredible quantities of rum, and molasses which has been distilled into rum among ourselves, have been imported; the most of which is consumed in intemperance and drunkenness in such a dreadful degree, as to exceed any thing of the kind in any part of the world; by which thousands, yea millions, have ruined themselves, body and soul, forever: Let any one consider this, and forbear to

*Hab. 2. 15.

confess, if he can, that this woe has fallen heavily upon us, and that in such a way and connection as to point out the sinful cause.

But to return. This trade has been carried on for a century and more, and for many years past, above an hundred thousand have been brought off the coast in a year, so that many, many millions have been torn from their native country, their acquaintance, relations and friends, and most of them put into a state of slavery, both themselves, and their children forever, if they shall have any posterity, much worse than death. When numbers of these wretched creatures are collected by the savages, they are bro't into the public market to be sold, all naked as they were born. The more than savage slave merchant views them, and sends his surgeon, more particularly to examine them, as to the soundness of their limbs, their age, &c. All that are passed as fit for sale, are branded with a hot iron in some part of their body, with the buyers mark; and then confined, crouded together in some close hold, till a convenient time to put them on board a ship. When they are bro't on board, all are immediately put in irons, except some of the women perhaps, and the small children, where they are so crouded together in that hot climate, that commonly a considerable number die on their passage to the *West-Indies*, occasioned partly by their confinement, partly by the grief and vexation of their minds, from the treatment they receive, and the situation in which they find themselves. And a number commonly die after they arrive at the *West-Indies*, in seasoning to the climate, so that commonly not above seventy in an hundred servive their transportation; by which means about thirty thousand are murdered every year by this slave trade, which amount to three millions in a century. When they are brought to the *West-Indies*, they are again exposed to market, as if they were so many beasts, and sold to the highest bidder; where again they are separated according to the humour of the traders, without any regard to their friendships or relations, of husbands and wives, parents and children, brothers and sisters, &c. being torn from each other, without the least regard to any thing of this kind, and sent to different places, without any prospect of seeing each other again. They are then put under task-masters, by the purchasing planter, who appoints them their work, and rules over them with rigor and cruelty, following them with his cruel whip, or appointing one to do it, if possible, more cruel than himself. The infirm and feeble, the females, and even those who are pregnant, or have infants to take care of, must do their task in the field equally with the rest; or if they fall behind, may be sure to feel the lash of their unmerciful driver. Their allowance of food at the same time is very coarse and scant, and must be cooked by themselves, if cooked at all, when they want to be asleep. And often they have no food but what they procure for themselves, by working on the sabbath; for that is the only time they have to themselves. And to make any complaint, or petition for relief, will expose them to some severe punishment, if not a cruel death. The least real or supposable crimes in them, are punished in the most cruel manner. And they have no relief; there being no appeal from their masters sentence and will, who commonly are more like savage beasts, than rational, humane creatures. And to petition for liberty, tho' in the most humble and modest terms, is as much as their lives are worth; as few escape the most cruel death, who presume to hint any thing of this kind to their masters: It being a maxim with those more than cruel tyrants, that the only way to keep them under, and prevent their thinking of the sweets of liberty, is to punish the least intimation of it in the severest manner, as the most intolerable affront and insult on their masters. Their labour is so hard, and their diet so scant and poor, and they are treated in all respects with such oppression and cruelty, that they do not increase by propagation in the islands, but constantly decrease, so that every planter must every year at least purchase five to every hundred he has on his plantation, in order to keep his number from diminishing.

But it is in vain to attempt a full description of the oppression and cruel treatment these poor creatures receive constantly at the hands of their imperious, unmerciful, worse than *Egyptian* taskmasters. Words cannot alter it. Volumes might be wrote, and not give a detail of a thousandth part of the shockingly cruel things they have suffered, and are constantly suffering. Nor can they possibly be conceived of by any one, who has not been an eye witness. And how little a part does he see! They who are witnesses to any part of this horrid scene of barbarous oppression, cannot but feel the truth and propriety of *Solomon's* words. "So I returned, and considered all the oppressions that are done under the sun: and behold the tears of the oppressed, and they had no comforter; and on the side of the oppressors there was power; but they had no comforter. Wherefore I praised the dead, which are already dead, more than the living which are yet alive."* *Solomon* never saw any oppression like this, unless he looked forward to this very instance, in the spirit of prophesy.

A. Sir, There is one important circumstance in favor of the slave trade; or which will at least serve to counterballance many of the evils you mention, and that is, we bring these slaves from a heathen land, to places of gospel light; and so put them under special advantages to be saved.

B. I know this has been mentioned by many in favor of the slave trade: but when examined, will turn greatly against it. It can hardly be said with truth, that the *West-India* islands are places of gospel light. But if they were, are the negroes in the least benefitted by it? Have they any access to the gospel? Have they the least instruction, more than if they were beasts? So far from this, that their masters guard against their having any instruction to their utmost; and if any one would attempt any such thing, it would be at the risk of his life. And all the poor creatures learn of Christianity, from what they see in those who call themselves Christians, only serves to prejudice them to the highest degree against the Christian religion. For they not only see the abominably wicked lives of most of those who are called Christians; but are constantly oppressed by them, and receive as cruel treatment from them, as they could from the worst of beings. And as to those who are brought to the continent, in the southern colonies, and even to *New-England,* so little pains are taken to instruct them, and there is so much to prejudice them against Christianity, that it is a very great wonder, and owing to an extraordinary divine interposition, in which we may say, God goes out of his common way, that any of them should think favorably of Christianity, and cordially embrace it. As to the most of them, no wonder they are unteachable, and get no good by the gospel; but have imbibed the deepest prejudices against it, from the treatment they receive from professed Christians; prejudices which most of them are by their circumstances restrained from expressing, while they are fixed in the strongest degree in their minds.

But if this was not the case, and all the slaves brought from *Africa,* were put under the best advantages to become Christians, and they

Eccl. 4. 1, 2.

were in circumstances that tended to give them the most favorable idea of Christians, and the religion they profess;* and tho' all concerned in this trade, and in slavery in general, should have this wholly in view, viz. their becoming Christians, by which they should be eternally happy; yet this would not justify the slave-trade, or continuing them in a state of slavery: For to take this method to christianize them, would be a direct and gross violation of the laws of Christ. He commands us to go and preach the gospel to all nations, to carry the gospel to them, and not to go, and with violence bring them from their native country, without saying a word to them, or to the nations from whom they are taken, about the gospel, or any thing that relates to it.

If the *Europeans* and *Americans* had been as much engaged to christianize the *Africans*, as they have been to enslave them; and had been at half the cost and pains to introduce the gospel among them, that they have to captivate and destroy them; we have all the reason in the world to conclude that extensive country, containing such a vast multitude of inhabitants, would have been full of gospel light, and the many nations there, civilized and made happy; and a foundation laid for the salvation of millions of millions; and the happy instruments of it have been rewarded ten thousand fold for all their labour and expence. But now, instead of this, what has been done on that coast, by those who pass among the Negroes for Christians,† has only served to produce and spread the greatest and most deep-rooted prejudices against the Christian religion, and bar the way to that which is above all things desirable, their coming to the knowledge of the truth that they might be saved. So that while, by the murdering or enslaving millions of millions, they have brought a curse on themselves, and on all that partake with them, they have injured in the highest degree innumerable nations, and done what they could to prevent their salvation, and to fasten them down in ignorance and barbarity to the latest posterity!—Who can realize all this, and not

---

*Which cannot be the case, so long as they are held in a state of slavery, or they brought away from their native country in the manner they are; so that the supposition is inconsistent, and destroys itself.

†For they have no way to get an idea of a Christian, but from the appearance and conduct of the Europeans or Americans, in the practice of all their unrighteousness, cruelty, profaneness and debauchery.

feel a mixture of grief, pity, indignation and horror, truly ineffable! And must he not be filled with zeal to do his utmost to put a speedy stop to this seven-headed monster of iniquity, with all the horrid train of evils with which it is attended.

And can any one consider all these things, and yet pretend to justify the slave-trade, or the slavery of the *Africans* in *America?* Is it not impossible, that a real Christian, who has attended to all this, should have any hand in this trade? And it requires the utmost stretch of charity to suppose that any one ever did, or can buy or sell an *African* slave, with a sincere view to make a true Christian of him.

A. All this seems to be little to the purpose; since it was granted in the beginning of our conversation, that the slave-trade, as it has been carried on, is not to be justified. But what is this to the question we proposed to consider; which is, Whether it be wrong to hold the blacks we have among us in a state of slavery, or ought to set them free without delay? To this you have said little or nothing as yet.

B. All I have said upon the slave-trade, to shew the unrighteousness, the cruelty, the murder, the opposition to Christianity and the spread of the gospel among the *Africans*, the destruction of whole nations, and myriads of souls, which are contained in this horrid practice, has been principally with a view to a more clear and satisfactory determination of the question before us, which you have now renewedly proposed.—For I think the following proposition may be advanced as undeniable, viz. *If the slave-trade is unjustifiable and wrong; then our holding the* Africans *and their children in bondage, is unjustifiable and wrong; and the latter is criminal in some proportion to the inexpressible baseness and criminality of the former:* For,

FIRST, If they have been brought into a state of slavery, by unrighteousness and violence, they having never forfeited their liberty, or given any one a right to enslave and sell them; then purchasing them of these piratical tyrants, and holding them in the same state of bondage into which they, contrary to all right, have brought them, is continuing the exercise of the same unrighteousness and violence towards them. They have yet as much a right to their liberty as ever they had, and to demand it of him who holds them in bondage; and he denies them their right, which is of more worth to them than every thing else they can have in the world, or all the riches the unjust master does or can possess; and therefore injures them in a very high degree every hour he refuses or neglects to set them at liberty. Besides,

Secondly, Holding these blacks in a state of slavery, is a practical justification of the slave-trade, and so brings the guilt of that on the head of him, who so far partakes in this iniquity, as to hold *one* of these a slave, who was unrighteously made so by these sons of violence. The old adage, "The partaker is as bad as the thief," carries such a plain truth in it, that every one must discern it: And it is certainly applicable to this case.

'Tis impossible to buy one of these blacks and detain him a slave, without partaking with him who first reduced him to this state, and put it in his power thus to possess him; and practically justifying him for so doing, so as to bring upon himself the guilt of first enslaving him. It is not therefore possible for any of our *slave keepers* to justify themselves in what they are doing, unless they can justify the slave trade: If they fail here, they bring on themselves an awful degree of the guilt of the whole.

Thirdly, By keeping these slaves, and buying and selling them, they actually encourage and promote the slave trade: And therefore, in this view, keeping slaves, and continuing to buy and sell them, is to bring on us the guilt of the slave trade, which is hereby supported. For so long as slaves are bought and possessed, and in demand; so long the *African* trade will be supported and encouraged....

4. Pennsylvania, An Act for the Gradual Abolition of Slavery (1780)

Pennsylvania, the center of American Quakerism, was the first political entity in the western world to legislate the gradual abolition of slavery. But Quakers were unpopular for their pacifism during the war and hence had to operate behind the scenes to obtain passage of the act. In this situation, the mantle of leadership in the antislavery struggle fell upon George Bryan, a Presbyterian and a member of the radical group in Pennsylvania that had displaced the conservative legislators in the last months before the Declaration of Independence. Bryan campaigned for the abolition law for several years, beginning in 1778, while the middle states were torn by war. But he had to make compromises to the slave owners of his state to secure passage of the law. In the final version, slave owners were able to retain the services of children born of slaves after March 1, 1780, until they were 28 years old rather than 21 years old, as the first draft of the bill specified. The preamble of the law expresses poignantly how Pennsylvanians developed a new sympathy for slaves because of the oppression of the British army toward the revolutionaries during its occupation of eastern Pennsylvania in 1777–1778.

An ACT for the gradual abolition of Slavery.

WHEN we contemplate our abhorrence of that condition to which the arms and tyranny of Great-Britain were exerted to reduce us; when we look back on the variety of dangers to which we have been exposed, and how miraculously our wants in many instances have been supplied, and our deliverances wrought, when even hope and human fortitude have become unequal to the conflict; we are unavoidably led to a serious and grateful sense of the manifold blessings which we have undeservedly received from the hand of that Being from whom every good and perfect gift cometh. Impressed with these ideas, we conceive that it is our duty, and we rejoice that it is in our power, to extend a portion of that freedom to others, which hath been extended to us; and a release from that state of thraldom, to which we ourselves were tyrannically doomed, and from which we have now every prospect of being delivered. It is not for us to inquire, why, in the creation of mankind, the inhabitants of the several parts of the earth were distinguished by a difference in feature or complexion. It is sufficient to know, that all are the work of an Almighty Hand. We find in the distribution of the human species, that the most fertile, as well as the most barren parts of the earth, are inhabited by men of complexions different from ours, and from each other, from whence we may reasonably, as well as religiously infer, that He, who placed them in their various situations, hath extended equally His care and protection to all, and that it becometh not us to counteract His mercies. We esteem it a peculiar blessing granted to us, that we are enabled this day, to add one more step to universal civilization, by removing as much as possible, the sorrows of those who have lived in undeserved bondage, and from which, by the assumed authority of the Kings of Britain, no effectual legal relief, could be obtained. Weaned by a long course of experience, from those narrow prejudices and partialities we had imbibed, we find our hearts enlarged with kindness and benevolence, towards men of all conditions and nations; and we conceive ourselves at this particular period extraordinarily called upon, by the blessings which we have received, to manifest the sincerity of our profession, and to give a substantial proof of our gratitude.

AND WHEREAS the condition of those persons who have heretofore been denominated Negroe and Mulatto slaves, has been attended with circumstances, which not only deprived them of the common blessings that they were by nature entitled to, but has cast them into the deepest afflictions, by an unnatural separation and sale of husband and wife from each other, and from their children; an injury the greatness of which, can only be conceived, by supposing, that we were in the same unhappy case. In justice therefore, to persons so unhappily circumstanced, and who, having no prospect before them, whereon they may rest their sorrows and their hopes, have no reasonable inducement, to render that service to society, which they otherwise might; and also, in grateful commemoration of our own happy deliverance, from that state of unconditional submission, to which we were doomed by the tyranny of Britain.

Be it enacted, and it is hereby enacted, by the Representatives of the Freemen of the Commonwealth of Pennsylvania, in General Assembly met, and by the authority of the same, That all persons, as well Negroes and Mulattos as others, who shall be born within this State, from and after the passing of this Act, shall not be deemed and considered as servants for life or slaves; and that all servitude for life, or slavery of children, in consequence of the slavery of their mothers, in the case of all children born within this State, from and after the passing of this Act as aforesaid, shall be, and hereby is utterly taken away, extinguished and for ever abolished.

Provided always, and be it further enacted by the authority aforesaid, That every Negroe and Mulatto child born within this State, after the passing of this Act as aforesaid, who would, in case this Act had not been made, have been born a servant for years, or life or a slave, shall be deemed to be and shall be by virtue of this Act, the servant of such person or his or her assigns, who would in such case have been intitled to the service of such child, until such child shall attain unto the age of twenty eight years, in the manner and on the conditions whereon servants bound by indenture for four years, are or may be retained and holden; and shall be liable to like correction and punishment, and intitled to like relief in case he or she be evily treated by his or her master or mistress, and to like freedom dues and other privileges as servants bound by indenture for four years, are or may be intitled, unless the person to whom the service of any such child shall belong, shall abandon his or her claim to the same, in which case the Overseers of the Poor of the city, township or district respectively, where such child shall be so abandoned, shall by indenture bind out every child so abandoned, as an apprentice for a time not exceeding the age herein before limited, for the service of such children. . . .

5. Virginia Manumission Law of 1782

Since 1723, it had been illegal for a private citizen to emancipate his or her slaves in Virginia. But in 1782, inspired by the revolutionary tide of opinion turning against slavery in America, the Virginia General Assembly authorized private manumissions. Thousands of slaves were set free in the following years with some slave owners, such as Robert Carter, freeing hundreds of slaves. A generation later, with the abolitionist spirit waning and the fear that free blacks were fanning the fires of slave insurrection, Virginia repealed the manumission law and reverted to the old prohibition against the private liberation of slaves.

An act to authorize the manumission of slaves.*

I. WHEREAS application hath been made to this present general assembly, that those persons who are disposed to emancipate their slaves may be empowered so to do, and the same hath been judged expedient under certain restrictions: *Be it therefore enacted,* That it shall hereafter be lawful for any person, by his or her last will and testament, or by any other instrument in writing, under his or her hand and seal, attested and proved in the county court by two witnesses, or acknowledged by the party in the court of the county where he or she resides, to emancipate and set free, his or her slaves, or any of them, who shall thereupon be entirely and fully discharged from the performance of any contract entered into during servitude, and enjoy as full freedom as if they had been particularly named and freed by this act.

II. *Provided always, and be it further enacted,* That all slaves so set free, not being in the judgment of the court, of sound mind and body, or being above the age of forty-five years, or being males under the age of twenty-one, or females under the age of eighteen years,

*William Waller Hening, ed., *The Statutes at Large; Being A Collection of All the Laws of Virginia* ... (13 vols., Richmond, 1823), XI, 39–40.

shall respectively be supported and maintained by the person so liberating them, or by his or her estate; and upon neglect or refusal so to do, the court of the county where such neglect or refusal may be, is hereby empowered and required, upon application to them made, to order the sheriff to distrain and sell so much of the person's estate as shall be sufficient for that purpose. *Provided also,* That every person by written instrument in his life time, or if by last will and testament, the executors of every person freeing any slave, shall cause to be delivered to him or her, a copy of the instrument of emancipation, attested by the clerk of the court of the county, who shall be paid therefor, by the person emancipating, five shillings, to be collected in the manner of other clerk's fees. Every person neglecting or refusing to deliver to any slave by him or her set free, such copy, shall forfeit and pay ten pounds, to be recovered with costs in any court of record, one half thereof to the person suing for the same, and the other to the person to whom such copy ought to have been delivered. It shall be lawful for any justice of the peace to commit to the gaol of his county, any emancipated slave travelling out of the county of his or her residence without a copy of the instrument of his or her emancipation, there to remain till such copy is produced and the gaoler's fees paid.

III. *And be it further enacted,* That in case any slave so liberated shall neglect in any year to pay all taxes and levies imposed or to be imposed by law, the court of the county shall order the sheriff to hire out him or her for so long time as will raise the said taxes and levies. *Provided* sufficient distress cannot be made upon his or her estate. *Saving nevertheless* to all and every person and persons, bodies politic or corporate, and their heirs and successors, other than the person or persons claiming under those so emancipating their slaves, all such right and title as they or any of them could or might claim if this act had never been made.

6. David Cooper, *A Serious Address to the Rulers of America, On the Inconsistency of their Conduct respecting Slavery* ... (Trenton, N. J., 1783)

"Ye pretended votaries for freedom! ye trifling patriots!" exclaimed the New England Baptist minister John Allen in 1774, "continuing this lawless, cruel, inhuman, and abominable practice of enslaving your fellow creatures." Allen's attack on the gross contradiction between waging a revolution based on inherent human rights while continuing to hold one-fifth of the population in bondage continued through the war years and into the early years of peace after 1783. David Cooper, a New Jersey Quaker, took up the antislavery cudgels and held back nothing in assaulting the hypocrisy of his fellow Americans in committing what he called "treason" against the natural rights of man and in making a mockery of the noble words of the Declaration of Independence. Anthony Benezet, only a year from his death, made sure that every member of the Congress received a copy of Cooper's biting pamphlet, printed here. (The copy of Cooper's pamphlet in the Boston Athenaeum is signed by George Washington, indicating that he had read this anti-slavery tract.)

A Sound mind in a sound body, is said to be a state of the highest human happiness individually; when these blessings are separate, a sound mind, wise and prudent conduct, tend much to support and preserve an unsound body: On the other hand, where the body is sound, the constitution strong and healthy, if the mind is unsound, the governing principle weak and feeble, the body feels the injuries which ensue, the health and constitution often become enfeebled and sickly, and untimely death closes the scene. This reasoning holds good politically, being sometimes realized in bodies politick, and perhaps never more so than in the conduct lately exhibited to mankind by Great-Britain. Her constitution was sound, strong and firm, in a degree that drew admiration from the whole world; but, for want of a sound mind, her directing and governing powers being imprudent and unwise, to such a debilitated and sickly state is this fine constitution reduced, that, without a change of regimen, her decease may not be very remote. America is a child of this parent, who long since, with many severe pangs, struggled into birth, and is now arrived to the state of manhood, and thrown off the restraints of an unwise parent, is become master of his own will, and, like a lovely youth, hath stepped upon the stage of action. State physicians pronounce his constitution strong and sound: the eyes of the world are singularly attentive to his conduct, in order to determine with certainty on the soundness of his mind. It is the general Congress, as the head, that must give the colouring, and stamp wisdom or folly on the counsels of America. May they demonstrate to the world, that these blessings, a sound mind in a sound body, are in America politically united!

I⊤ was a claim of freedom unfettered from the arbitrary control of others, so essential to free agents, and equally the gift of our beneficent Creator to all his rational children, which put fleets and armies into motion, covered earth and seas with rapine and carnage, disturbed the repose of Europe, and exhausted the treasure of nations. Now is the time to demonstrate to Europe, to the whole world, that America was in earnest, and meant what she said, when, with peculiar energy, and unanswerable reasoning, she plead the cause of human nature, and with undaunted firmness insisted, that *all mankind* came from the hand of their Creator *equally free*. Let not the world have an opportunity to charge her conduct with a contradiction to her solemn and often repeated declarations; or to say that her sons are not real friends to freedom; that they have been actuated in this awful contest by no higher motive than selfishness and interest, like the wicked servant in the gospel, who, after his Lord had forgiven his debt which he was utterly unable to pay, shewed the most cruel severity to a fellow servant for a trifling demand, and thereby brought on himself a punishment which his conduct justly merited. Ye rulers of America beware: Let it appear to future ages, from the records of this day, that you not only professed to be advocates for freedom, but really were inspired by the love of mankind, and wished to secure the invaluable blessing to all; that, as you disdained to submit to the unlimited control of others, you equally abhorred the crying crime of holding your fellow men, as much entitled to freedom as yourselves, the subjects of your undisputed will and pleasure.

HOWEVER habit and custom may have rendered familiar the degrading and ignominious distinctions, which are made between people with a black skin and ourselves, I am not ashamed to declare myself an advocate for the rights of that highly injured and abused people; and were I master of all the resistless persuasion of Tully and Demosthenes, could not employ it better, than in vindicating their rights as men, and forcing a blush on every American slaveholder, who has complained of the treatment we have received from Britain, which is no more to be equalled, with ours to negroes, than a barley corn is to the globe we inhabit. Must not every generous foreigner feel a secret indignation rise in his breast when he hears the language of Americans upon any of their own rights as freemen, being in the least infringed, and reflects that these very people are holding thousands and tens of thousands of their innocent fellow men in the most debasing and abject slavery, deprived of every right of freemen, except light and air? How similar to an atrocious pirate, setting in all the solemn pomp of a judge, passing sentence of death on a petty thief. Let us try the likeness by the standard of facts.

THE first settlers of these colonies emigrated from England, under the sanction of royal charters, held all their lands under the crown, and were protected and defended by the parent state, who claimed and exercised a control over their internal police, and at length attempted to levy taxes upon them, and, by statute, declared the colonies to be under their jurisdiction, and that they had, and ought to have, a right to make laws to bind them in all cases whatsoever.

AFRICA lies many thousand miles distant, its inhabitants as independent of us, as we are of them; we sail there, and foment wars among them in order that we may purchase the prisoner, and encourage the stealing one another to sell them to us; we bring them to America, and consider them and their posterity forever, our slaves, subject to our arbitrary will and pleasure; and if they imitate our example, and offer by force to assert their native freedom, they are condemned as traitors, and a hasty gibbet strikes terror on their survivors, and rivets their chains more secure.

THE American Congress in their declaration, July 1775, say,

"IF it were *possible* for men who exercise their reason to believe that the divine Author of our existence intended a *part* of the human race to hold an absolute property in, and an unbounded power over others, marked out by infinite goodness and wisdom, as the objects of a legal domination never rightly resistible, however severe and oppressive; the inhabitants of these colonies might at least require from the parliament of Great-Britain some evidence, that this *dreadful authority* over them has been granted to that body. But a *reverence* for our *great Creator, principles of humanity*, and the dictates of *common sense*, must convince all those who reflect upon the subject, that government was instituted to promote the welfare of mankind, and ought to be administered for the attainment of that end."

AGAIN they say,—"By this perfidy (Howe's conduct in Boston) *wives* are *separated* from their *husbands, children* from their *parents*, the aged and sick from their *relations* and *friends*, who wish to attend and *comfort* them."

DOES not this forcible reasoning apply equally to Africans? Have we a better right to enslave them and their posterity, than Great-Britain had to demand Three-pence per pound for an article of luxury we could do very well without? And Oh! America, will not a *reverence* for our *great Creator, principles* of *humanity*, nor the *dictates* of *common sense*, awaken thee to *reflect*, how far thy government falls short of impartially *promoting* the *welfare* of *mankind*, when its laws suffer, yea justify men in murdering, torturing and abusing their fellow men, in a manner shocking to humanity?

How abundantly more aggravated is our conduct in these respects to Africans, in bringing them from their own country, and separating by sale these near connections, never more to see each other, or afford the least *comfort* of tender endearment of social life. But they are black, and ought to obey; we are white, and ought to rule.—Can a better reason be given for the distinction, that Howe's conduct is *perfidy*, and ours innocent and blameless, and justified by our *laws?*

"WE most solemnly before GOD and the world declare, that exerting the utmost energy of those powers which our beneficent Creator hath graciously bestowed upon us, the arms we have been compelled by our enemies to assume, we will in defiance of every *hazard*, with unabated firmness and perseverance, employ for the preservation of our liberties, being with one mind resolved to die freemen rather than live *slaves.*"

THOU wicked servant, out of thine own mouth shalt thou be judged.—Is a claim to take thy property without thy consent so galling, that thou wilt defy every hazard rather than submit to it? And at the same time hold untold numbers of thy fellow men in slavery, (which robs them of every thing valuable in life) as *firmly riveted* by *thee*, as thou art resolved to use the utmost energy of thy power, to preserve thy own freedom?

"WE exhibit to mankind the remarkable spectacle of a people attacked by *unprovoked enemies*, without any imputation, or even suspicion, of offence.—They boast of their privileges and civilization, and yet proffer no milder conditions than servitude or death."

HAVE the Africans offered us the least *provocation* to make us their *enemies?*—Have their infants committed, or are they even *suspected* of any offence? And yet we leave them no alternative but *servitude* or *death*.

"IN our own native land, in defence of the freedom that is our birthright, and which we ever enjoyed till the late violation of it; for the protection of our property acquired solely by the

THE unenlightened Africans, in their own native land, enjoyed freedom which was their birthright, until the more savage christians transported them by thousands, and sold them for

121

honest industry of our fore-
fathers and ourselves; against violence actually offered, we have
taken up arms."

IN a resolve of Congress,
October 1774, they say,

"THAT the Inhabitants of the
English colonies in North-Amer-
ica, by the *immutable laws of nature*, are entitled to life, liberty
and property; and they have
never ceded to any sovereign
power whatever a right to dispose of either without their consent."

To the people of Great-Britain.

"KNOW then that we consider
ourselves, and do insist, that we
are and ought to be, as free as our
fellow-subjects in Britain, and
that no power on earth has a right
to take our property from us
without our consent."

"ARE the proprietors of the
soil of America less lords of their
property than you are of yours?
&c.—Reason looks with indignation on such distinctions, and
freemen can never perceive their
propriety; and yet, however, chi-
merical and unjust such discrim-
inations are; the Parliament assert, that they have a right to bind
us in all cases without exception,

slaves in the wilds of America, to
cultivate it for their lordly oppressors.

WITH equal justice may negroes say, By the *immutable laws
of nature*, we are equally entitled
to life, liberty and property with
our lordly masters, and have
never *ceded* to any power whatever, a *right* to deprive us thereof.

DOES this reasoning apply
more forcibly in favour of a
white skin than a black one?
Why ought a negro to be less
free than the subjects of Britain,
or a white face in America? Have
we not all one father? Hath not
one God created us? Why do we
deal treacherously every man
against his brother? Mal. ii. 10.

Do Americans reprobate this
doctrine when applied to themselves? And at the same time enforce it with ten-fold rigor upon
others, who are indeed *pensioners*
on their *bounty* for all they *possess*,
nor can they *hold* a single enjoyment of life longer than they
vouchsafe to *permit*?

whether we consent or not; that they may take and use our property when and in what manner they please; that we are pensioners on their bounty for all we possess, and can hold it no longer than they vouchsafe to permit."

IF neither the *voice of justice,* the dictates of the law, the principles of the constitution, or the *suggestions* of *humanity,* can restrain your hands from shedding human blood in such an *impious* cause: we must then tell you, that we never will submit to be hewers of wood or drawers of water for any ministry or nation on earth. And in future, let *justice* and *humanity* cease to be the boast of your nation."

To the inhabitants of the colonies.

"WEIGH in the opposite balance, the endless miseries you and your descendants must endure, from an established arbitrary power."

Declaration of independence in Congress, 4th July, 1776.

"WE hold these truths to be self-evident, that *all men* are created *equal,* that they are endowed

YOU who have read a description of the inhuman scenes occasioned by the slave-trade, in *obtaining, branding, transporting, selling,* and keeping in *subjection* millions of human creatures; reflect a moment, and then determine which is the most *impious cause*: and after this, if neither the *voice of justice* nor suggestions of *humanity,* can *restrain* your *hands* from being contaminated with the practice; cease to *boast* the christian name from him who commanded his followers "to do unto others as they would others should do unto them."

WHO would believe the same persons whose feelings are so exquisitely sensible respecting themselves, could be so callous toward negroes, and the *miseries* which, by their *arbitrary power,* they wantonly inflict.

IF these solemn *truths,* uttered at such an awful crisis, are *self-evident*: unless we can shew that the African race are not *men,* words can hardly express the by their Creator with certain *un-alienable rights*; that among these are *life*, *liberty*, and the *pursuit* of *happiness*."

Declaration of rights of Pennsylvania, July 15, 1776.

"THAT *all men* are born *equally free* and *independent*, and have certain natural inherent, and *unalienable rights*, among which are, the enjoying and defending *life* and *liberty*, acquiring, possessing and protecting *property*, and pursuing and obtaining happiness and safety."

Declaration of rights of Massachusetts, Sep. 1, 1779.

"*All men* are born *free* and *equal*, and have certain natural essential and *unalienable rights*; among which may be reckoned the right of enjoying and defending their *lives* and *liberties*; that of acquiring, possessing and protecting *property*; in fine, of seeking and obtaining *safety* and *happiness*."

amazement which naturally arises on reflecting, that the very people who make these pompous declarations are slave-holders, and, by their legislative conduct, tell us, that these blessings were only meant to be the *rights* of *whitemen* not of *all men*: and would seem to verify the observation of an eminent writer; "When men talk of liberty, they mean their own liberty, and seldom suffer their thoughts on that point to stray to their neighbours."

THIS was the voice, the language of the supreme council of America, in vindication of their rights as men, against imposition and unjust control:—Yes, it was the voice of all America, through her representatives in solemn Congress uttered. How clear, full and conclusive! "We hold these truths to be self-evident, that all men are created equal, and endowed by their Creator with the unalienable rights of life, liberty and the pursuit of happiness." "By the immutable laws of nature *all men* are entitled to life and liberty." We need not now turn over the libraries of Europe for authorities to prove that blacks are born equally free with whites; it is declared and recorded as the sense of America: Cease then ye cruel taskmasters, ye petty tyrants, from attempting to vindicate your having the same interest in your fellow men as in your cattle, and let blushing and confusion of face strike every American, who henceforth shall behold advertisements offering their brethren to sale, on a footing with brute beasts.

BUT what shall I say! Forgive it, Oh Heaven, but give ear, Oh earth! while we are execrating our parent state with all the bitterness of invective, for attempting to abridge our freedom, and invade our property; we are holding our brethren in the most servile bondage, cast out from the *benefit* of our *laws*, and subjected to the cruel treatment of the most imperious and savage tempers, without *redress*, without advocate or friend.

OUR rulers have appointed days for humiliation, and offering up of prayer to our common Father to deliver us from *our* oppressors, when sighs and groans are piercing his holy ears from oppressions which we commit a thousand fold more grievous: pouring forth blood and treasure year after year in defence of our own *rights*; exerting the most assiduous attention and care to secure them by laws and sanctions, while the poor Africans are continued in chains of slavery as creatures unworthy of notice in these high concerns, and left subject to laws disgraceful to humanity, and opposite to every precept of christianity. One of these in effect gives Fifteen Pounds for the murder of a slave; that is, after a slave has absconded a certain time, Twenty Pounds is given to any one who shall bring his head, and but Five Pounds if he is brought alive. Another, which empowers certain officers to seize negroes set free, and sell them for the benefit of government: And, even during the present contest, negroes have been seized with the estates of persons who had gone over to the British, and sold by publick auction into *perpetual slavery*, and the proceeds cast into stock for the *defence* of American *liberty*. Of the same complexion is an instance in New-Jersey: A female Quaker, about seven years since, manumitted her negroes; the times having reduced her so as to be unable fully to discharge a debt for which she was only surety, the creditor, a great declaimer in behalf of *American freedom*, although he was offered his principal money, obtains a judgment, levies on these free negroes, who by the assistance of some real friends of freedom, procured a *habeas corpus*, and removed their case before the justices of the supreme court. How many such mock patriots hath this day discovered, whose flinty hearts are as impervious to the tender feelings of humanity and commiseration as the nether millstone; can sport with the rights of men; wallow and riot in the plunder, which their unhallowed hands have squeezed from others! But only touch *their* immaculate interests, and what an unceasing outcry invades every ear. A love for my country, a regard for the honour of America, raises an ardent wish, that this picture may never be realized in her rulers.

IT may be objected that there are many difficulties to be guarded against in setting of negroes free, and that, were they all to be freed at once, they would be in a worse condition than at present. I admit that there is some weight in these objections; but are not these difficulties of our own creating? And must the innocent continue to suffer because we have involved ourselves in difficulties? Let us do justice as far as circumstances will admit, give such measure as we ask, if we expect Heaven to favour us with the continuance of our hard earned liberty. The work must be begun, or it can never be completed. "It is begun and many negroes are set free." True, it is begun, but not in a manner likely to produce the desired *end*, the entire *abolition* of *slavery*. This is the business of the superintending authority, the main spring which gives motion to the whole political machine; which, were they to undertake in good earnest, I have no doubt but we should soon see a period fixed, when our land should no longer be polluted with slave-holders, nor give forth her increase to feed slaves: And indeed it hath been a matter of wonder to many, that that body, who have been so much employed in the study and defence of the *rights* of *humanity*, should suffer so many years to elapse without any effectual movement in this business. Had they, with the declaration of independence, recommended it to the different Legislatures to provide laws, declaring, that no person imported into, or born in America after that date, should be held in slavery; it would have been a step correspondent with our own *claims*, and in time, have completed the work, nor can I see any impropriety, but what the nature of the case will justify, to have it still take place.

To shew the necessity of this matter taking its rise at the head, if any thing effectual is done, I may instance the Quakers. Some among them, it is said, always bore a testimony against slavery from its first introduction, and the uneasiness increasing, advices were given forth cautioning their members against being concerned in importing slaves, to use those well whom they were possessed of, school their children, &c. but some of the foremost of that society having experienced the profits of their labour, no effectual stop could be put to the practice, tho' many became uneasy, and set their negroes free, until the difficulties attending the late French and Indian war, brought the rights of men into a more close inspection, when a rule was agreed upon, prohibiting their members from being concerned with importing, buying, or selling of slaves; and some years after a further rule was made, enjoining all those who held slaves to set them free, otherwise to be separated from religious membership.—The work was then soon accomplished, and they now say there are very few members belonging to the yearly meeting of Philadelphia who hold a slave.

WHEN a grievance is general, it is but trifling to apply partial means; it is like attempting to destroy a great tree by nibbling at its branches. It is only the supreme power which pervades the whole that can take it up by the roots.—The disquisitions and reasonings of the present day on the rights of men, have opened the eyes of multitudes who clearly see, that, in advocating the rights of humanity, their slaves are equally included with themselves, and that the arguments which they advance to convict others, rebounds with redoubled force back on themselves, so that few among us are now hardy enough to justify slavery, and yet will not release their slaves; like hardened sinners, acknowledge their guilt, but discover no inclination to reform. It is true these convictions have occasioned the release of many slaves, and two or three states to make some feeble efforts looking that way; but I fear, after the sunshine of peace takes place, we have little more to expect, unless the sovereign power is exerted to finish this sin, and put an end to this crying transgression.

LET me now address that august body, who are by their brethren clothed with sovereign power, to sit at the helm, and give a direction to the important concerns of the American union. You, gentlemen, have, in behalf of America, *declared* to Europe, to the world, "That all men are born *equal,* and, by the *immutable laws* of *nature,* are *equally* entitled to liberty." We expect, mankind expects, you to demonstrate your *faith* by your *works;* the *sincerity* of your *words* by your *actions,* in giving the *power,* with which you are *invested,* its utmost *energy* in promoting *equal* and *impartial* liberty to *all* whose lots are cast within the reach of its influence—then will you be revered as the real friends of mankind, and escape the execrations which pursue human tyrants, who shew no remorse at sacrificing the ease and happiness of any number of their fellow-men to the increase and advancement of their own, are wholly regardless of others rights if theirs are but safe and secure. We are encouraged in this expectation by the second article of your nonimportation agreement in behalf of America, October 1774, *viz.* "That we will neither import nor purchase any slave imported after the first day of December next, after which time we will wholly discontinue the slave-trade, and will neither be concerned in it ourselves, nor will we hire our vessels nor sell our commodities or manufactures to those who are concerned in it."—And much would it have been for the honour of America, had it been added and confirmed by laws in each state (nor will we suffer such a stigma to remain on our land, as that it can produce slaves, therefore no child, born in any of the United States after this date, shall be held in slavery.)—But the children of slaves are private property, and cannot be taken from their masters without a compensation! What! After it hath so often been echoed from America, "All men are born equally free." "No man or body of men can have a legitimate property in, or control over their fellow-men, but by their own consent expressed or implied. Shall we now disown it in order to hold our slaves? Forbid it all honest men; it is treason against the rights of humanity, against the principles upon which the American revolution stands, and by which the present contest can only be justified; to deny it, is to justify Britain in her claims, and declare ourselves rebels. Wherefore our rulers undoubtedly ought to give these principles, these laws which themselves have declared *immutable,* a due force and efficacy. This every wellwisher to their country, either in a religious or political sense have a right to ask and expect. But we have laws that will maintain us in the possession of our slaves: "The fundamental law of nature being the good of mankind, no human sanctions can be good, or valid against it, but are of themselves void, and ought to be resisted," Lock[e]. Therefore none can have just cause of complaint, should so desirable an event take place, as that no person brought into, or born within any of the United States after the declaration of independence, shall be held a slave.

WHEN I read the constitutions of the different states, they afford a mournful idea of the partiality and selfishness of man; the extraordinary care, and wise precautions they manifest to guard and secure our own rights and privileges, without the least notice of the injured Africans, or gleam of expectation afforded them, of being sharers of the golden fruitage, except in that of the Delaware state, who, to their lasting honour, while they were hedging in their own, provided against the invasion of the rights of others. By the twenty-sixth article of their constitution they resolve, that "No person hereafter imported into this state from Africa, ought to be held in slavery under any pretence whatever; and no negro, indian or mulatto slave, ought to be brought into this state for sale from any part of the world." Had they went further and made provision by which slavery must at length have terminated within their jurisdiction, it would have been doing something to the purpose; and, as this is the only constitution in which posterity will see any regard paid to that abused people, I hope the same humane considerations which led them so far, will induce them to take the lead* in doing their part toward putting an effectual end to this crying evil, which will ever remain a stain to the annals of America.

AND you who in the several states are clothed with legislative authority, and have now an opportunity of displaying your wisdom and virtue by your laws freed from every foreign control, although this people were below notice, and their rights and interest thought unworthy of a sanction in your constitutions; let me beseech you, if you wish your country to escape the reproach and lasting infamy of denying to others what *she* hath so often, and in the most conclusive language, declared were the rights of *all*; if you wish to retain the name of christians, of friends to human nature, and of looking up

---

*When this was written I had, by information, been led to believe, that the late Pennsylvania slave law was very partial and inadequate, but have since learned, that it is a judicious and well constructed law, which provides for the entire abolition of slavery in that state.

acceptably in prayer to the common father of men to deal with you
in the same tenderness and mercy as you deal with others; that you
would even now regard the rigorous oppressions of his other children,
and your brethren, which they suffer under laws which you only can
abrogate. View your negro laws calculated not to protect and defend
them, but to augment and heighten their calamitous situation! Cast
out and rejected by the regulations formed for the defence and security of the rights and privileges, and to guard and improve the
morals and virtue of the whites: Left open to the gratification of
every passion and criminal commerce with one another, as though
they were brutes and not men; fornication, adultery, and all the rights
of marriage union among blacks, considered beneath the notice of
those rules and sanctions formed to humanize and restrain corrupt
nature, or the regard of those whose duty it is to enforce them. Yes,
blush Americans! Ye have laws, with severe penalties annexed, against
these crimes when committed between whites; but, if committed by
blacks, or by white men with black women, with the aggravated
circumstances of force and violence, they pass as subjects of mirth,
not within the cognizance of law or magistrates inquiry, and lose the
very name of crimes. Hence children often become familiar with
these scenes of corruption and wickedness, before they are capable
of distinguishing between the duties of christianity, and the appetites
of unrestrained nature. No marvel then if slave-holders are often
scourged by the vices of their own offspring, which their untutored
slaves have been a means of inflicting—children who, instead of being
educated in the nurture and admonition of the Lord, are too often
nurtured in pride, idleness, lewdness, and the indulgence of every
natural appetite; that, were there no other inducement, this singly is
sufficient to cause every real christian to lift a hand against, and exert
their utmost influence in, bringing this hydra mischief to a period.
But when we consider the accumulated guilt, in other respects, abundantly set forth by other writers on this subject, brought on this land
through the introduction of this infernal traffick, at a time when we
were denied the privilege of making laws to check the mighty evil;
and that near ten years have now elapsed since this restraint hath
been removed, and no effectual advance yet made towards loosing
the bands of wickedness, and letting the oppressed go free, or even
of putting it in a train whereby it may at length come to an end; I

say, it is matter of anxious sorrow, and affords a gloomy presage to the true friends of America. Have we reason to expect, or dare we ask of him whose *ways* are all *equal*, the continuance of his blessings to us, whilst our *ways* are so *unequal*.

I shall now conclude with the words of Congress to the people of England, a little varied to suit the present subject.

"IF neither the voice of *justice*, the dictates of *humanity*, the *rights* of *human nature*, and establishment of *impartial liberty now in your power*, the good of your *country*, nor the fear of an *avenging God*, can restrain your hands from this *impious practice* of holding your fellowmen in *slavery*; making traffick of, and advertising in your publick prints for sale as common merchandize, *your brethren* possessed of immortal souls equal with yourselves; then let *justice, humanity, advocates for liberty*, and the sacred name of *christians*, cease to be the *boast* of *American rulers*."

A FARMER.

February, 1783.

Documents for Chapter 2

THE FAILURE OF ABOLITIONISM

I. Consider Arms, Malichi Maynard, and Samuel
Field, "Reasons for Dissent to the Federal
Constitution," Northampton, Mass., *Hampshire
Gazette*, April 16, 1788

Although the Constitutional Convention had side-
stepped the issue of abolishing slavery in the summer
of 1787, and, in fact, had provided important constitutional supports for the institution, some political voices
could not be silenced on the controversial topic. From
western Massachusetts, where the Shays rebels had
raised a rebellion against eastern mercantile policy just
a year before, came a ringing denunciation of the Constitution for allowing the continuation of the slave trade
and for failing to put a stop to slavery altogether. "This
practice of enslaving mankind" the three authors wrote,
"is in direct opposition to a fundamental maxim of truth,
on which our state constitution is founded, viz. 'All
men are born free and equal.'" Of the hundreds of
published arguments urging that Americans not ratify

the Constitution, only a few criticized it for its toleration of slavery. Already the high-water mark of the revolutionary generation's antislavery sentiment seemed to be receding.

For the HAMPSHIRE GAZETTE.

Conclusion of Messrs. ARMS's, MAYNARD's and FIELD's Reasons for giving their Dissent to the Federal Constitution.

But we pass on to another thing, which (aside from every other consideration) was, and still is an insuperable objection in the way of our assent. This we find in the 9th section under the head of restrictions upon Congress, viz. "The migration or importation of such persons as any of the states now existing shall think proper to admit, shall not be prohibited by the Congress, prior to the year one thousand eight hundred and eight," &c. It was not controverted in the Convention, but owned that this provision was made purely that the southern states might not be deprived of their profits arising from that most *nefarious trade* of enslaving the Africans. The hon Mr. King himself, who was an assistant in forming this constitution, in discoursing upon the slave trade, in the late Convention at Boston, was pleased to design it by this epithet, *nefarious*, which carries with it the idea of something peculiarly wicked and abominable: and indeed we think it deserving of this and every odious epithet which our language affords, descriptive of the iniquity of it. This being the case, we were naturally led to enquire why we should establish a constitution, which gives licence to a measure of this sort—How is it possible we could do it consistent with our ideas of government? consistent with the principles and documents we endeavour to inculcate upon others? It is a standing law in the kingdom of Heaven, "Do unto others as ye would have others do unto you." This is the royal law—this we often hear inculcated upon others. But had we given our affirmative voice in this case, could we have claimed to ourselves that consistent line of conduct, which marks the path of every honest man? Should we not rather have been guilty of a contumelious repugnancy, to what we profess to believe is equitable and just? Let us for once bring the matter home to ourselves, and summons up our own feelings upon the occasion, and hear the simple sober verdict of our own hearts, were we in the place of those unhappy Africans—this is the test, the proper *touch-stone* by which to try the matter before us. Where is the man, who under the influence of sober dispassionate reasoning, and not void of natural affection, can lay his hand upon his heart and say, I am willing my sons and my daughters should be torn from me and doomed to perpetual slavery? We presume that man is not to be found amongst us: And yet we think the consequence is fairly drawn, that this is what every man ought to be able to say, who voted for this constitution. But we dare say this will never be the case here, so long as the country has power to repel force by force. Notwithstanding this we will practise this upon those who are destitute of the power of repulsion: from whence we conclude it is not the tincture of a skin, or any disparity of features that are necessarily connected with slavery, and possibly may therefore fall to the lot of some who voted it, to have the same measure measured unto them which they have measured unto others. If we could once make it our own case, we should soon discover what distress & anxiety, what poignant feelings it would produce in our own breasts, to have our infants torn from the bosoms of their tender mothers—indeed our children of all ages, from infancy to manhood, arrested from us by a banditti of lawless ruffians, in defiance of all the laws of humanity, and carried to a country far distant, without any hope of their return—attended likewise with the cutting reflection, that they were likely to undergo all those indignities, those miseries, which are the usual concomitants of slavery. Indeed when we consider the depredations committed in Africa, the cruelties exercised towards the poor captivated inhabitants of that country on their passage to this—crowded by droves into the holds of ships, suffering what might naturally be expected would result from scanty provisions, and inelastic infectious air, and after their arrival, drove like brutes from market to market, *branded* on their naked *bodies* with *hot irons* with the initial letters of their masters names—fed upon the entrails of beasts like swine in the slaughter-yard of a butcher; and many other barbarities, of which we have documents well authenticated: then put to the hardest of labour, and to perform the vilest of drudges—their masters (or rather *usurpers*) by far less kind and benevolent to them, than to their horses and their hounds. We say, when we consider these things (the recollection of which gives us pain) conscience applauds the decision we have made, and we feel that satisfaction which arises from acting agreeable to its dictates. When we hear those barbarities pled for—When we see them voted for, (as in the late Convention at Boston) when we see them practised by those who denominate themselves Christians, we are presented with something truely *heterogeneous*—something *monstrous* indeed! Can we suppose this line of conduct keeps pace with the rule of right? Do such practices coincide with the plain and simple ideas of government before-mentioned? By no means. We could wish it might be kept in mind, that the very notion of government is to protect men in the enjoyment of those privileges to which the[y] have a natural, therefore an indefeasible right; and not to be made an engine of rapine, robbery and murder. This is but establishing inequity, by law founded on usurpation. Establishing this constitution is, in our opinion, establishing the most ignominious kind of theft, man-stealing, and so heinous and agrivated was this crime considered, by ONE who cannot err, that under the Jewish theocracy it was punished with death. Indeed what can shew men scarcely more hardened, than being guilty of this crime? for there is *nothing else* they will stick at in order to perpetrate this.

The question therefore—Why should we vote for the establishment of this system? recoils upon us armed with treple force—force which sets at defiance, the whole power of sophistry, employed for the defence of those, who by a "cursed thirst for gold," are prompted on to actions, which cast an indelible stain upon the character of the human species—actions at which certain quadrupeds, were they possessed of Organs for the purpose, would discover a BLUSH.

But we were told by an honourable gentleman who was one of the framers of this Constitution, that the two southernmost states, absolutely refused to confederate at all, except they might be gratified in this article. What then? Was this an argument sufficient to induce us to give energy to this article, thus fraught with inequity? By no means. But we were informed by that gentleman, further that those two states pled, that they had lost much of their property during the late war. Their slaves being either taken from them by the British troops, or they themselves taking the liberty of absconding from them, and therefore they must import more, in order to make up their losses. To this we say they lost no property, because they never had any in them, however much money they might have paid for them. For we look upon it, every man is the sole proprietor of his own liberty, and no one but himself hath a right to convey it unless by some crime adequate to the punishment, it should be made forfeit, and so by that means becomes the property of government: But this is by no means the case in the present instance. And we cannot suppose a vendee, can acquire property in any thing, which at the time of purchase, he knew the vendor had no right to convey. This is an acknowledgment, we are constrained to make as a tribute due to justice and equity. But suppose they had lost real property; so have we; and indeed where is the man, but will tell us he has been a great loser by means of the war? And shall we from thence argue that we have a right to make inroads upon another nation, pilfer and rob them, in order to compensate ourselves for the losses we have sustained by means of a war, in which they have been utterly neutral? Truly upon this plan of reasoning it is lawful thus to do, and had we voted the constitution as it stands, we must have given countenance to conduct equally criminal, and more so, if possible. Such arguments as the above seem to be calculated and designed for idiotcy. We however acknowledge, we think them rather an affront, even upon that.

The hon. Gentleman above named, was asked the question— What would be the consequence, suppose one or two states, upon any principle, should refuse confederating? His answer was—"The consequence is plain and easy—they would be compelled to it; not by force of arms; but all commerce with them would be interdicted; and their property would be seized in every port they should enter, and by law made forfeit: and this line of conduct would soon reduce them to order." This method of procedure perhaps no one would be disposed to reprehend; and if eleven, or even nine states were agreed, could they not, ought they not to take this method, rather than to make a compact with them, by which they give countenance, nay even bind themselves (as the case may be) to aid and assist them in spor[t]ing with the liberties of others, and accumulating to themselves fortunes, by making thousands of their fellow creatures miserable. To animadvert upon the British manoevres at that time, would not fall within the compass of our present design. But that the Africans had a right to depart, we must assert, and are able to prove it from the highest authority perhaps that this Commonwealth does or ever did afford. In a printed pamphlet, published in Boston in the year 1772, said to be the report of a Committee, and unanimously voted by said town, and ordered to be sent to the several towns in the state for their consideration. In said pamphlet we find the following *axiom*, which we will quote verbatim,—page 2d—"All men have a right to remain in a state of nature as long as they please, and in case of intolerable oppression, civil or religious, to leave the society they belong to, and enter into another." If it can by any kind of reasoning be made to appear, that this authority is not pertinently adduced in the case before us, then we think it can by the same reasoning be investigated, that black is white and white is black—that oppression and freedom are exactly similar, and benevolence and malignity synonomous terms.

The advocates for the constitution seemed to suppose, that this restriction being laid upon Congress only for a term of time, is the "fair dawning of liberty." That "it was a glorious acquisition towards the final abolition of slavery." But how much more glorious would the acquisition have been, was such abolition to take place the first moment the constitution should be established. If we had said that after the expiration of a certain term the practice should cease, it would have appeared with a better grace; but this is not the case, for even after that, it is wholly optional with the Congress, whether they abolish it or not. And by that time we presume the enslaving the Africans will be accounted by far less an inconsiderable affair than it is at present: therefore conclude from good reasons, that the '*nefarious practice*' will be continued and increased as the inhabitants of the country shall be found to increase.

This practice of enslaving mankind is in direct opposition to a fundamental maxim of truth, on which our state constitution is founded, viz. "All men are born free and equal." This is our motto. We have said it—we cannot go back. Indeed no man can justify himself in enslaving another, unless he can produce a commission under the broad seal of Heaven, purporting a licence therefor from him who created all men, and can therefore dispose of them at his pleasure.

We would not be thought to detract from the character of any person, but to us it is somewhat nearly paradoxical, that some of our leading characters in the law department (especially in the western counties) after having (to their honour be it spoken) exerted themselves to promote, and finally to effect the emancipation of slaves, should now turn directly about, and exhibit to the world principles diametrically opposite thereto: that they should now appear such strenuous advocates for the establishment of that diabolical trade of importing the Africans. But said some, it is not we who do it—and compared it to entering into an alliance with another nation, for some particular purpose; but we think this by no means a parallel. We are one nation, forming a constitution for the whole, and suppose the states are under obligation, whenever this constitution shall be established, reciprocally to aid each other in defence and support of every thing to which they are entitled thereby, right or wrong. Perhaps we may never be called upon to take up arms for the defence of the southern states, in prosecuting this abominable traffick.

It is true at present there is not much danger to be apprehended, and for this plain reason are those innocent Africans (as to us) pitched upon to drag out their lives in misery and chains. Such is their local situation—their unpolished manners—their inexperience in the art of war, that those invaders of the rights of mankind know they can, at present, perpetrate those enormities with impunity. But let us suppose for once, a thing which is by no means impossible, viz. that those Africans should rise superior to all their local and other disadvantages, and attempt to avenge themselves for the wrongs done them? Or suppose some potent nation should interfere in their behalf, as France in the cause of America, must we not rise and resist them? Would not the Congress immediately call forth the whole force of the country, if needed, to oppose them, and so attempt more closely to rivet their manacles upon them, and in that way perpetuate the miseries of those unhappy people? This we think the natural consequence which will flow from the establishment of this constitution, and that it is not a forced, but a very liberal construction of it. It was said that "the adoption of this Constitution, would be ominous of much good, and betoken the smiles of Heaven upon the country." But we view the matter in a very different light; we think this lurch for unjust gains, this lust for slavery, portentous of much evil in

America, for the cry of innocent blood, which hath been shed in carrying on this execrable commerce, hath undoubtedly reached to the Heavens, to which that cry is always directed, and will draw down upon them vengeance adequate to the enormity of the crime. To what other cause, than a full conviction, of the moral evil in this practice, together with some fearful forebodings of punishment therefor arising in the minds of the Congress in the year 1774, can it be imputed, that drew from them at that time, (at least an implied) confession of guilt, and a solemn, explicit promise of reformation? This is a fact, but lest it should be disputed, we think it most safe for ourselves to lay before our readers, an extract from a certain pamphlet, entitled "Extracts from the votes and proceedings of the American Continental Congress, held at Philadelphia, on the 5th of September, 1774, &c." In the 22d page of this same pamphlet, we find the following paragraph, viz. "Second. That we will neither import, nor purchase any slave imported, after the first day of December next; after which time we will wholly discontinue the slave-trade, and will neither be concerned in it ourselves, nor will we hire our vessels nor sell our commodities or manufactures to those who are concerned in it." The inconsistency of opposing slavery, which they thought designed for themselves, and by clandestine means, procuring others to enslave at the same time—it is very natural to suppose would stare them in the face, and at all times guard them against breaking their resolution. Hence it appears to us unaccountable strange, that any person who signed the above resolve, should sign the federal constitution. For do they not hold up to view principles diametrically opposite? Can we suppose that what was morally evil in the year 1774, has become in the year 1788, morally good? Or shall we change evil into good and good into evil, as often as we find it will serve a turn? We cannot but say the conduct of those who associated in the year 1774 in the manner above, and now appear advocates for this new constitution, is highly inconsistent, although we find such conduct has the celebrated names of a *Washington* and an *Adams* to grace it. And this may serve as a reason why we could not be wrought upon by another argument, which was made use of in the Convention in favour of the constitution, viz. *the weight of names*—a solid argument with some people who belonged to the Convention, and would have induced them to comply with measures of almost any kind. It was urged that the gentlemen who composed the federal Convention, were men of the greatest abilities, integrity and erudition, and had been the greatest contenders for freedom. We suppose it to be true, and that they have exemplified it, by the manner in which they have earnestly dogmatized for liberty—But notwithstanding we could not view this argument, as advancing any where towards infallibility—because long before we entered upon the business of the Convention, we were by some means or other possessed with a notion (and we think from good authority) that *"great men are not always wise."* And to be sure the weight of a name adduced to give efficacy to a measure where liberty is in dispute, cannot be so likely to have its intended effect, when the person designed by that name, at the same time he is brandishing his sword, in the behalf of freedom for himself—is likewise tyranizing over two or three hundred miserable Africans, as free born as himself.

In fine we view this constitution as a curious piece of political mechanism, fabricated in such manner as may finally despoil the people of all their privileges; and we are fully satisfied, that had the same system been offered to the people in the time of the contest with Great-Britain, the person offering the same would not have met the approbation of those who now appear the most strenuous advocates for it. We cannot slip this opportunity of manifesting our disgust at the unfair methods which were taken in order to obtain a vote in this state, which perhaps was the means of producing the *small* majority of *nineteen*, out of nearly three hundred and sixty members. What those methods were is well known. It is past dispute that the opposers of the constitution were, in sundry instances, treated in a manner utterly inconsistent with that respect which is due to every freeborn citizen of the commonwealth, especially when acting in the capacity of a representative.

Notwithstanding what has been said, we would not have it understood, that we mean to be disturbers of the peace, should the states receive the constitution; but on the contrary, declare it our intention, as we think it our duty, to be subject to "the powers that be," wherever our lot may be cast.

CONSIDER ARMS,   } Conway.
MALICHI MAYNARD, }
SAMUEL FIELD, Deerfield.

2. Luther Martin, "Genuine Information," Baltimore *Maryland Gazette*, January 22, 1788

Luther Martin, attorney general of Maryland, was one of the most outspoken critics of slavery. Martin was one of Maryland's delegates at the Constitutional Convention. Deciding to oppose ratification of the Constitution, he composed a series of essays, *Genuine Information*, by which he hoped to convince the people of Maryland to reject the Constitution. Martin's essays were reprinted in many newspapers, from South Carolina to Massachusetts, and compiled in a widely circulated pamphlet. Thus, this excerpt from "Genuine Information" attacking slavery and the slave trade was widely read, and it is all the more important because it came from the hand of a prominent southerner and a member of the Constitutional Convention. Martin's *Genuine Information* also remains an important source for learning about the secret debates of the Convention.

Mr. MARTIN's *Information to the House of Assembly, continued.*

It was urged that by this system, we were giving the general government full and absolute power to regulate commerce, under which general power it would have a right to *restrain*, or *totally prohibit* the *slave trade*—it must appear to the world absurd and disgraceful to the last degree, that we should except from the exercise of that power, the *only branch* of *commerce*, which is *unjustifiable in its nature*, and *contrary* to the *rights* of *mankind*—That on the contrary, we ought *rather to prohibit expressly* in our *constitution*, the *further importation* of *slaves*; and to *authorize* the general government from time to time, to make such regulations as should be thought most advantageous for the *gradual abolition* of *slavery*, and the *emancipation* of the *slaves* which are already in the States.

That *slavery* is *inconsistent* with the *genius* of *republicanism*, and has a tendency to *destroy* those *principles* on which it is *supported*, as it *lessens the sense* of the *equal rights* of *mankind*, and habituates us

to *tyranny* and *oppression.*—It was further urged, that by this system
of government, every State is to be protected both from *foreign invasion* and from *domestic insurrections*; that from this consideration,
it was of the *utmost importance* it should have a power to restrain
the importation of slaves, since in *proportion* as the number of slaves
were encreased in any State, in the *same* proportion the State is
weakened and *exposed* to foreign invasion, or domestic insurrection,
and *by so much the less* will it be able to protect itself against *either*;
and therefore will by so much the more, want aid from, and be a
burthen to, the union.—It was further said, that as in this system we
were giving the general government a power under the idea of national character, or national interest, to regulate even our *weights* and
measures, and have prohibited all possibility of *emitting paper money*,
and *passing instalment laws, &c.*—It must appear still more extraordinary, that we should prohibit the government from interfering with
the slave trade, than which *nothing* could so *materially affect* both
our *national honour* and *interest.*—These reasons influenced me both
on the committee and in convention, most decidedly to oppose and
vote against the clause, as it now makes a part of the system.

You will perceive, Sir, not only that the general government is
prohibited from interfering in the slave trade *before* the year eighteen
hundred and eight, but that there is no provision in the constitution
that it shall *afterwards* be prohibited, nor any security that such prohibition will ever take place—and I think there is great reason to
believe that if the importation of slaves is permitted until the year
seventeen [*sic*] hundred and eight, it will not be prohibited afterwards—
At *this time* we do not generally hold this commerce in so *great*
abhorrence as we have done.—When our *own* liberties were at stake,
we *warmly* felt for the *common rights of men*—The danger being
thought to be past, which threatened ourselves, we are daily growing
more insensible to those rights—In those States who have restrained
or prohibited the importation of slaves, it is only done by legislative
acts which may be repealed—When those States find that they must
in their *national character* and *connection* suffer in the *disgrace*, and
share in the *inconveniences* attendant upon that detestable and iniquitous traffic, they may be desirous also to share in the *benefits* arising
from it, and the odium attending it will be greatly effaced by the
sanction which is given to it in the general government....

3. Petition from Pennsylvania Abolition Society to Congress (1790)

Founded just a few days after the British and Americans clashed at Concord and Lexington in 1775, the Pennsylvania Abolition Society was the first antislavery society in the western world. It worked to end the foreign slave trade, to abolish slavery, and to assist emancipated slaves in their efforts to find jobs, an education, and social justice. After ratification of the Constitution in 1788, the Society lobbied with Congress to stop the slave trade, even though the Constitution itself prohibited Congress from banning the trade before 1808. It also urged Congress to use its powers to ameliorate the worst excesses of the slave system. With Philadelphia Quakers playing the key roles, the Abolition Society petitioned the second session of the first Congress in February 1790. The petition was signed by Benjamin Franklin, the Society's president, then less than a year from death.

That from a regard for the happiness of Mankind, an Association was formed several years since in this State by a number of her Citizens, of various religious denominations for promoting the *Abolition of Slavery* & for the relief of those unlawfully held in bondage. A just and accurate Conception of the true Principles of liberty, as it spread through the land, produced accessions to their numbers, many friends to their Cause, & a legislative Co-operation with their views, which, by the blessing of Divine Providence, have been successfully directed to the *relieving from bondage a large number of their fellow Creatures of the African Race*. They have also the Satisfaction to observe, that in consequence of that Spirit of Philanthropy & genuine liberty which is generally diffusing its beneficial Influence, similar Institutions are gradually forming at home & abroad.

That mankind are all formed by the same Almighty being, alike objects of his Care & equally designed for the Enjoyment of Happiness the Christian Religion teaches us to believe, & the Political Creed of Americans fully coincides with the Position. Your Memorialists, particularly engaged in attending to the Distresses arising from Slavery, believe it their indispensible Duty to present this Subject to your notice—They have observed with great Satisfaction, that many important & salutary Powers are vested in you for "promoting the Welfare & *securing the blessings of liberty to the People of the United States.*" And as they conceive, that these blessings ought rightfully to be administered, *without distinction of Colour*, to all descriptions of People, so they indulge themselves in the pleasing expectation, that nothing, which can be done for the relief of the unhappy objects of their care will be either omitted or delayed—

From a persuasion that equal liberty was originally the Portion, & is still the Birthright of all Men, & influenced by the strong ties of Humanity & the Principles of their Institution, your Memorialists conceive themselves *bound to use all justifiable endeavours to loosen the bands of Slavery* and promote a general Enjoyment of the blessings of Freedom. Under these Impressions they earnestly intreat your serious attention to the Subject of Slavery, that you will be pleased to countenance the *Restoration of liberty* to those unhappy Men, who alone, in this land of Freedom, are degraded into perpetual Bondage, and who, amidst the general Joy of surrounding Freemen, are groaning in Servile Subjection, that you will devise means for removing this *Inconsistency from the Character of the American People*; that you will promote Mercy and Justice towards this distressed Race, & that you will Step to the very verge of the Powers vested in you for discouraging every Species of Traffick in the Persons of our fellow Men.

B. Franklin
Presidt. of the Society

Philadelphia, *Feby.* 3d. 1790.

4. Ferdinando Fairfax, "Plan for Liberating the Negroes within the United States," *American Museum* (December, 1790)

The first detailed plan for a general emancipation of American slaves came from an upper-class member of the state with the largest slave population. Ferdinando Fairfax was a wealthy Virginia planter and slaveowner with close connections to George Washington. An earlier plan for a compensated emancipation in Connecticut had been conceived in 1775 by Levi Hart of Southington, Connecticut, but his "Thoughts on Abolition" had never been published. Now, in late 1790, Fairfax published his plan in Philadelphia, the city to which the federal government had just moved from New York City. Fairfax's insistence that emancipation would have to be accompanied by the removal of free blacks to a new colony in Africa became a standard feature of almost all later emancipation schemes. Moreover, his reasons for regarding it as impossible for blacks and whites to live together were echoed in virtually all succeeding essays on the subject.

Plan for liberating the negroes within the united states. By mr. Ferdinando Fairfax.

This subject has afforded, in conversation, a wide field for argument, or rather, speculation, both to the friends and opposers of emancipation. Whilst the former plead natural right and justice, which are considered as paramount to every other consideration: the latter insist upon policy, with respect both to the community and to those who are the objects proposed to be benefited: the one party considers liberty as a natural right, which we cannot, without injustice, withhold from this unhappy race of men: the other, at the same time that it admits these principles, opposes a general emancipation, on account of the inconveniencies which would result to the community and to the slaves themselves, and which, consequently, would render it impolitic; besides the injustice which would be done to individuals by a legislative interference (without voluntary consent) in private property, which had been acquired and possessed under the laws of the country. But no practicable scheme has yet been proposed, which would unite all these principles of justice and policy, and thereby remove all ground for opposition: all that has hitherto been offered to the public upon this subject, has been addressed, rather to the feelings, than to the cool and deliberate judgment. The following plan is therefore submitted, without apology, since it is only intended to suggest the idea, which may be improved by some abler hand.

It seems to be the general opinion, that emancipation must be gradual; since, to deprive a man, at once, of all his right in the property of his negroes, would be the height of injustice, and such as, in this country, would never be submitted to: and the resources of government are by no means adequate to making at once a full compensation. It must therefore be by voluntary consent—consequently in a gradual manner. It is equally agreed, that, if they be emancipated, it would never do to allow them *all* the privileges of citizens: they would therefore form a separate interest from the rest of the community. There is something very repugnant to the general feelings, even in the thought of their being allowed that free intercourse, and the privilege of intermarriage with the white inhabitants, which the other freemen of our country enjoy, and which only *can* form one common interest. The remembrance of their former situation, and a variety of other considerations, forbid this privilege—and as a proof, where is the man of all those who have liberated their slaves, who would marry a son or a daughter to one of them? and if *he* would not, who would? So that these prejudices, sentiments, or whatever they may be called, would be found to operate so powerfully as to be insurmountable. And though the laws should allow these privileges, yet the same effect would still be produced, of forming a separate interest from the rest of the community; for the laws cannot operate effectually against the sentiments of the people.

If this separate interest of so great a number in the same community, be once formed, by any means, it will endanger the peace of society: for it cannot exist between two neighbouring states, without danger to the peace of each—How much less, then, between the inhabitants of the same country?

This suggests the propriety, and even necessity of removing them to a distance from this country. It is therefore proposed,

That a colony should be settled, under the auspices and protection of congress, by the negroes now within the united states, and be composed of those who already, as well as those who, at any time hereafter, may become liberated by the voluntary consent of their owners; since there are many who would willingly emancipate their slaves, if there should appear a probability of their being so disposed of, as neither to injure themselves nor the community. As an additional inducement, government may, as the resources of the country become greater, offer a reward or compensation, for emancipation. There is, however, in the mean time, a sufficient number to form a very considerable colony.

That congress should frame a plan, and appoint the proper officers for the government of the colony in its infant state, until the colonists should themselves become competent to that business.

That there should be suitable provision made for their support and defence. And

That, to forward their progress in the useful arts, and to qualify them for the business of legislation; a considerable number of those who are intended to be sent over after the first settlement, should be properly educated and instructed; and that one of the first objects should be the establishment of seminaries in the colony for a like purpose.

That the seat of this colony should be in Africa, their native climate, as being most suitable for the purposes intended. They will there be at such a distance as to prevent all the before-mentioned inconveniences of intercourse, &c. at the same time that they are situated within the neighbourhood of other nations of the same kind of people, with whom they may, after a little time, maintain the most intimate intercourse without any inconvenience. They will still have a great superiority over their neighbours, on account of their knowledge in the several useful arts, and as they gradually advance in importance, will, by their influence, diffuse this knowledge among this rude race of men. Nor ought we to consider as of little importance, the tendency that this settlement would have, to spreading a knowledge of the christian religion among so great a proportion of mankind, who are at present ignorant of it—and that too in the most effectual manner.

With respect to ourselves, we might reap every advantage that we could enjoy from the settlement of any other colony—if not more. They would require our support and protection for a short time only, with fewer supplies of necessaries than any other (from the nature of the climate). And they might soon, from their industry, and by commercial intercourse, make us ample amends for our expenses, and be enabled to live without our protection; and, after some time, to become an independent nation. But if we should gain no advantages, we should still accomplish the object intended.

Many difficulties and objections may be urged against this plan; but none, that are not equally forcible against the first planting of any other colony; and had they been fully admitted, neither this country, nor any other colony, would ever have been settled.

It may be said, that England, not long since, made an experiment of this kind, which was found not to succeed. But this can, by no means, be admitted as decisive: the number they sent over, was very small, compared to what we should be able to send: and perhaps, the means they adopted were incompetent to the accomplishment of the object. But did not the same thing occur in the first settlement of Virginia? There were two attempts made, before they succeeded; nor did the colony, at last, begin to flourish, until proper encouragements were given to industry, by the prospect presented to each man, individually, of receiving the reward of this industry, by commercial intercourse with other countries, and by the benefit which would result immediately to himself or to his family. This is confirmed by a circumstance recorded in the history of this colony, viz. when they first began to labour for subsistence, the plan was, that the produce of each man's labour, should be put into the common stock, from whence all should be supplied as occasion required. The consequence was, that they never made enough for their support, and were once or twice near starving; but as soon as each man had his own ground assigned him, with directions to maintain himself and family, they made a plenty.

It may, however, be urged, that the negroes (having contracted such dispositions for idleness as always to require compulsion) will never voluntarily labour for subsistence. It is granted, that this would be the case, where they to remain among us, where they find other means of support, and where they may prey upon others: and it is even probable, that, for a little time after their removal, the force of habit would operate in a considerable degree. But there can be no doubt, but that the same circumstances, which have once influenced mankind in any situation, will, in the same situation, actuate them again. And let us consult human nature—we shall find, that no man would labour but through necessity, or, after this necessity is answered, wtihout some stimulus to honour or grandeur, either to himself or to his posterity: and that there is hardly any man who will not, from some of these motives, be induced to industry, if placed in a situation where there is no other resource.

All these motives are now wanting to the people in question: but who can say that when, by a change of situation, they shall operate in their full force, they will not have their effect?

Richmond, March 6, 1790.

5. St. George Tucker, *A Dissertation on Slavery: With a Proposal for the Gradual Abolition of It, in the State of Virginia* (Philadelphia, 1796)

St. George Tucker came to Virginia from Bermuda on the eve of the Revolution and soon earned a place as a respected member of the Tidewater aristocracy. He became a judge of the Virginia Supreme Court of Appeals and a professor of law at the College of William and Mary, where he was apparently much influenced by the antislavery professor George Wythe. The long pamphlet he published in Philadelphia in 1796, excerpted here, proposed a very gradual abolition of slavery—over the course of a century, in fact—in a complicated system that would free only female slaves and their children and would never allow free blacks the civil privileges that were the automatic right of white Virginians. By the time Tucker published the pamphlet, the fear that the American South would be infected by the slave insurrection in St. Domingue, which had been raging since 1791, was very much in the mind of all who thought about the problems of slavery. Tucker's ideas were first worked out in lectures delivered at the College of William and Mary. We have no way of knowing how the ideas expressed here affected the sons of upper-class Virginians who attended the college.

ON THE
STATE OF SLAVERY IN VIRGINIA.

In the preceding Enquiry *(a)* into the absolute rights of the citizens of united America, we must not be understood as if those rights

(a) The subject of a preceding Lecture, with which the present was immediately connected, was, An Enquiry into the Rights of Persons, as Citizens of the United States of America.

were equally and universally the privilege of all the inhabitants of
the United States, or even of all those, who may challenge this land
of freedom as their native country. Among the blessings which the
Almighty hath showered down on these states, there is a large portion
of the bitterest draught that ever flowed from the cup of affliction.
Whilst America hath been the land of promise to Europeans, and
their descendants, it hath been the vale of death to millions of the
wretched sons of Africa. The genial light of liberty, which hath here
shone with unrivalled lustre on the former, hath yielded no comfort
to the latter, but to them hath proved a pillar of darkness, whilst it
hath conducted the former to the most enviable state of human existence. Whilst we were offering up vows at the shrine of Liberty,
and sacrificing hecatombs upon her altars; whilst we swore irrec-
oncilable hostility to her enemies, and hurled defiance in their faces;
whilst we adjured the God of Hosts to witness our resolution to live
free, or die, and imprecated curses on their heads who refused to
unite with us in establishing the empire of freedom; we were imposing upon our fellow men, who differ in complexion from us, a
slavery, ten thousand times more cruel than the utmost extremity of
those grievances and oppressions, of which we complained. Such are
the inconsistencies of human nature; such the blindness of those who
pluck not the beam out of their own eyes, whilst they can espy a
moat, in the eyes of their brother; such that partial system of morality
which confines rights and injuries, to particular complexions; such
the effect of that self-love which justifies, or condemns, not according
to principle, but to the agent. Had we turned our eyes inwardly when
we supplicated the Father of Mercies to aid the injured and oppressed;
when we invoked the Author of Righteousness to attest the purity
of our motives, and the justice of our cause; and implored the God
of Battles to aid our exertions in its defence, should we not have
stood more self convicted than the contrite publican! Should we not
have left our gift upon the altar, that we might be first reconciled to
our brethren whom we hold in bondage? Should we not have loosed
their chains, and broken their fetters? Or if the difficulties and dangers of such an experiment prohibited the attempt during the convulsions of a revolution, is it not our duty to embrace the first moment
of constitutional health and vigour, to effectuate so desirable an object,
and to remove from us a stigma, with which our enemies will never

fail to upbraid us, nor our consciences to reproach us? To form a just estimate of this obligation, to demonstrate the incompatability of a state of slavery with the principles of our government, and of that revolution upon which it is founded, and to elucidate the practicability of its total, though gradual, abolition, it will be proper to consider the nature of slavery, its properties, attendants, and consequences in general; its rise, progress, and present state not only in this commonwealth, but in such of our sister states as have either perfected, or commenced the great work of its extirpation; with the means they have adopted to effect it, and those which the circumstances and situation of our country may render it most expedient for us to pursue, for the attainment of the same noble and important end.

...Were we even to admit, that a captive taken in a *just war*, might by his conqueror be reduced to a state of slavery, this could not justify the claim of Europeans to reduce the natives of Africa to that state: it is a melancholy, though well-known fact, that in order to furnish supplies of these unhappy people for the purposes of the slave trade, the Europeans have constantly, by the most insidious (I had almost said infernal) arts, fomented a kind of perpetual warfare among the ignorant and miserable people of Africa; and instances have not been wanting, where, by the most shameful breach of faith, they have trepanned and made slaves of the *sellers* as well as the *sold*. That such horrid practices have been sanctioned by a civilized nation; that a nation ardent in the cause of liberty, and enjoying its blessings in the fullest extent, can continue to vindicate a right established upon such a foundation; that a people who have declared, "That *all men* are by nature *equally free* and *independent*," and have made this declaration the first article in the foundation of their government, should in defiance of so sacred a truth, recognized by themselves in so solemn a manner, and on so important an occasion, tolerate a practice incompatible therewith, is such an evidence of the weakness and inconsistency of human nature, as every man who hath a spark of patriotic fire in his bosom must wish to see removed from his own country. If ever there was a cause, if ever an occasion, in which all hearts should be united, every nerve strained, and every power exerted, surely the restoration of human nature to its inalienable right is such: Whatever obstacles, therefore, may hitherto have retarded the attempt, he that can appreciate the honour and happiness of his country, will think it time that we should attempt to surmount them. . . .

From this view of our jurisprudence respecting slaves, we are unavoidably led to remark, how frequently the laws of nature have been set aside in favour of institutions, the pure result of prejudice, usurpation, and tyranny. We have found actions, innocent, or indifferent, punishable with a rigour scarcely due to any, but the most atrocious, offences against civil society; justice distributed by an unequal measure to the master and the slave; and even the hand of mercy arrested, where mercy might have been extended to the wretched culprit, had his complexion been the same with that of his judges: for, the short period of ten days, between his condemnation and execution, was often insufficient to obtain a pardon for a slave, convicted in a remote part of the country, whilst a free man, condemned at the seat of government, and tried before the governor himself, in whom the power of pardoning was vested, had a respite of thirty days to implore the clemency of the executive authority.—It may be urged, and I believe with truth, that these rigours do not proceed from a sanguinary temper in the people of Virginia, but from those political considerations indispensibly necessary, where slavery prevails to any great extent: I am moreover happy to observe that our police respecting this unhappy class of people, is not only less rigorous than formerly, but perhaps milder than in any other country where there are so many slaves, or so large a proportion of them, in respect to the free inhabitants: it is also, I trust, unjust to censure the present generation for the existence of slavery in Virginia: for I think it unquestionably true, that a very large proportion of our fellow-citizens lament that as a misfortune, which is imputed to them as a reproach; it being evident from what has been already shewn upon the subject, that, *antecedent to the revolution*, no exertion to abolish, or even to check the progress of, slavery, in Virginia, could have received the smallest countenance from the crown, without whose assent the united wishes and exertions of every individual here, would have been wholly fruitless and ineffectual: it is, perhaps, also demonstrable, that at no period since the revolution, could the abolition of slavery in this state have been safely undertaken until the foundations of our newly established governments had been found capable of supporting the fabric itself, under any shock, which so arduous an attempt might have produced. But these obstacles being now happily removed, considerations of policy, as well as justice and humanity, must evince the necessity of eradicating the evil, before it becomes impossible to do it, without tearing up the roots of civil society with it. . . .

The plan therefore which I would presume to propose for the consideration of my countrymen is such, as the number of slaves, the difference of their nature, and habits, and the state of agriculture, among us, might render it *expedient*, rather than *desirable* to adopt: and would partake partly of that proposed by Mr. Jefferson, and adopted in other states; and partly of such cautionary restrictions, as a due regard to situation and circumstances, and even to *general* prejudices, might recommend to those, who engage in so arduous, and perhaps unprecedented an undertaking.

1. Let every female born after the adoption of the plan be free, and transmit freedom to all her descendants, both male and female.

2. As a compensation to those persons, in whose families such females, or their descendants may be born, for the expence and trouble of their maintenance during infancy, let them serve such persons until the age of twenty-eight years: let them then receive twenty dollars in money, two suits of clothes, suited to the season, a hat, a pair of shoes, and two blankets. If these things be not voluntarily done, let the county courts enforce the performance, upon complaint.

3. Let all Negroe children be registered with the clerk of the county or corporation court, where born, within one month after their birth: let the person in whose family they are born take a copy of the register, and deliver it to the mother, or if she die to the child, before it is of the age of twenty-one years. Let any Negroe claiming to be free, and above the age of puberty, be considered as of the age of twenty-eight years, if he or she be not registered, as required.

4. Let all such Negroe servants be put on the same footing as white servants and apprentices now are, in respect to food, raiment, correction, and the assignment of their service from one to another.

5. Let the children of Negroes and mulattoes, born in the families of their parents, be bound to service by the overseers of the poor, until they shall attain the age of twenty-one years.—Let all above that age, who are not housekeepers, nor have voluntarily bound them-

selves to service for a year before the first day of February annually, be then bound for the remainder of the year by the overseers of the poor. Let the overseers of the poor receive fifteen per cent. of their wages, from the person hiring them, as a compensation for their trouble, and ten per cent. per annum out of the wages of such as they may bind apprentices.

6. If at the age of twenty-seven years, the matter of a Negroe or mulattoe servant be unwilling to pay his freedom dues, above mentioned, at the expiration of the succeeding year, let him bring him into the county court, clad and furnished with necessaries as before directed, and pay into court five dollars, for the use of the servant, and thereupon let the court direct him to be hired by the overseers of the poor for the succeeding year, in the manner before directed.

7. Let no Negroe or mulattoe be capable of taking, holding, or exercising, any public office, freehold, franchise or privilege, or any estate in lands or tenements, other than a lease not exceeding twenty-one years.—Nor of keeping, or bearing arms, unless authorised so to do by some act of the general assembly, whose duration shall be limitted to three years. Nor of contracting matrimony with any other than a Negroe or mulattoe; nor be an attorney; nor be a juror; nor a witness in any court of judicature, except against, or between Negroes and mulattoes. Nor be an executor or administrator; nor capable of making any will or testament; nor maintain any real action; nor be a trustee of lands or tenements himself, nor any other person to be a trustee to him or to his use.

8. Let all persons born after the passing of the act, be considered as entitled to the same mode of trial in criminal cases, as free Negroes and mulattoes are now entitled to.

The restrictions in this place may appear to favour strongly of prejudice: whoever proposes any plan for the abolition of slavery, will find that he must either encounter, or accommodate himself to prejudice.—I have preferred the latter; not that I pretend to be wholly exempt from it, but that I might avoid as many obstacles as possible to the completion of so desirable a work, as the abolition of slavery. Though I am opposed to the banishment of the Negroes, I wish not to encourage their future residence among us. By denying them the most valuable privileges which civil government affords, I wished to render it their inclination and their interest to seek those privileges in some other climate. There is an immense unsettled territory on this continent more congenial to their natural constitutions than ours, where they may perhaps be received upon more favourable terms than we can permit them to remain with us. Emigrating in small numbers, they will be able to effect settlements more easily than in large numbers; and without the expence or danger of numerous colonies. By releasing them from the yoke of bondage, and enabling them to seek happiness wherever they can hope to find it, we surely confer a benefit, which no one can sufficiently appreciate, who has not tasted of the bitter curse of compulsory servitude. By excluding them from offices, the seeds of ambition would be buried too deep, ever to germinate: by disarming them, we may calm our apprehensions of their resentments arising from past sufferings; by incapacitating them from holding lands, we should add one inducement more to emigration, and effectually remove the foundation of ambition, and party-struggles. Their personal rights, and their property, though limited, would whilst they remain among us be under the protection of the laws; and their condition not at all inferior to that of the *labouring* poor in most other countries. Under such an arrangement we might reasonably hope, that time would either remove from us a race of men, whom we wish not to incorporate with us, or obliterate those prejudices, which now form an obstacle to such incorporation.

But it is not from the want of liberality to the emancipated race of blacks that I apprehend the most serious objections to the plan I have ventured to suggest.—Those slave holders (whose numbers I trust are few) who have been in the habit of considering their fellow creatures as no more than cattle, and the rest of the brute creation, will exclaim that they are to be deprived of their *property*, without compensation. Men who will shut their ears against this moral truth, that all men are by nature *free*, and *equal*, will not even be convinced that they do not possess a *property* in an *unborn* child: they will not distinguish between allowing to *unborn* generations the absolute and unalienable rights of human nature, and taking away that which they *now possess*; they will shut their ears against truth, should you tell them, the loss of the mother's labour for nine months, and the maintenance of a child for a dozen or fourteen years, is amply compensated by the services of that child for as many years more, as he has been an expence to them. But if the voice of reason, justice and humanity be not stifled by sordid avarice, or unfeeling tyranny, it would be easy to convince even those who have entertained such erroneous notions, that the right of one man over another is neither founded in nature, nor in sound policy. That it cannot extend to those *not in being*; that no man can in reality be *deprived* of what he doth not possess: that fourteen years labour by a young person in the prime of life, is an ample compensation for a few months of labour lost by the mother, and for the maintenance of a child, in that coarse homely manner that Negroes are brought up: And lastly, that a state of slavery is not only perfectly incompatible with the principles of government, but with the safety and security of their masters. History evinces this. At this moment we have the most awful demonstrations of it. Shall we then neglect a duty, which every consideration, moral, religious, political, or *selfish*, recommends. Those who wish to postpone the measure, do not reflect that every day renders the task more arduous to be performed. We have now 300,000 slaves among us. Thirty years hence we shall have double the number. In sixty years we shall have 1,200,000. And in less than another century from this day, even that enormous number will be doubled. Milo acquired strength enough to carry an ox, by beginning with the ox while he was yet a calf. If we complain that the calf is too heavy for our shoulders, what will not the ox be?

To such as apprehend danger to our agricultural interest, and the depriving the families of those whose principal reliance is upon their slaves, of support, it will be proper to submit a view of the gradual operation, and effects of this plan. They will no doubt be surprized to hear, that whenever it is adopted, the number of slaves will not be diminished for forty years after it takes place; that it will even encrease for thirty years; that at the distance of sixty years, there will be one-third of the number at its first commencement: that it will require *above a century* to complete it; and that the number of blacks *under twenty-eight*, and consequently bound to service, in the families they are born in, will always be at least as great, as the present number of slaves. These circumstances I trust will remove many objections, and that they are truly stated will appear upon enquiry. . . .

6. George Tucker, *A Letter to a Member of the General Assembly . . . with a Proposal for Colonization* (Baltimore, 1801)

The St. Domingue black rebellion that began in 1791 had frightened southerners badly because by this time the South contained nearly 700,000 slaves—many of them potential insurrectionists. With the discovery of Gabriel Prosser's intended insurrection in Richmond, Virginia, in 1800, southern fears of black rebellion grew even stronger. "The late extraordinary conspiracy has set the public mind in motion: it has waked those who were asleep, and wiped the film from the eyes of the blind," he wrote in the pamphlet excerpted here. Like his cousin, St. George Tucker, George Tucker found slavery a rankling sore and a contradiction of the republicanism on which the country's political and social system was built. And like St. George Tucker, he called for emancipation and removal—but this time to the western parts of the United States (not yet extended by the Louisiana Purchase).

SIR,

THE services you have more than once rendered your country; the opinions you are known to entertain on domestic slavery; and above all, the sacred duty you owe to those who appointed you to the station you now fill, are the considerations which induce me to trouble you with this letter. The high importance of the subject, and the lively interest it excites, are the only apologies I can offer for writing it. By you, I trust, they will be deemed sufficient.

YOU must have observed, sir, that some truths, which their self-evidence and importance have rendered familiar to the mind, are, on this very account, often disregarded.—Nobody remarks on what every body sees; and that which we have long known is not likely to impress the mind with much force. Of this nature, is the danger arising from domestic slavery. Every man is persuaded of the reality of this danger;

no man denies its magnitude; but his opinion has as little influence on his conduct, and excites as little emotion in his mind, as the belief of rewards and punishments, in the next world, influences human conduct in this.

IT is true, the late extraordinary conspiracy has set the public mind in motion: it has waked those who were asleep, and wiped the film from the eyes of the blind. The ignorant and the philosophic agree in considering it as an awful alarm of a future danger, which may involve the dearest interests of their country. But these apprehensions are the short-lived creatures of a day: suddenly excited, they will as suddenly yield to the tempting repose of a false and fatal security. Men are blind, lamentably blind, to distant evils. As the mole-hill that is near occupies a greater portion of our view than the distant mountain, so, in the scale of human appreciation, the mite of present inconvenience outweighs a mighty mass of that which is remote.

THIS propensity is the more to be lamented, as it is always easier to prevent than to remedy; and it is sometimes easy to prevent what it becomes afterwards impossible to remedy. The overthrow of the Grecian states was forseen, and might have been averted, by unanimity in their councils. Had the Roman senate listened to the prophetic warnings of Cato, Caesar had never trampled on the liberties of his country. Happy for Virginia, if the guardians of her welfare will act with that wisdom and decision which the occasion demands, and which they have so often displayed on less serious emergencies.

WHILE all agree that our danger is great and certain, various are the opinions of the nature and extent of the remedy to be applied. Some are for palliating what they think admits not of a radical cure; whilst others, more bold, and perhaps more cautious too, are for laying the axe to the root, and at once extirpating this growing evil. For my part, sir, I freely confess to you, I consider it as an eating sore, which will yield only to the knife, or the caustic; and that it is far better to submit to the pain of the operation, than to endanger the life of the state. I will lay before you the grounds on which I have formed my opinion.

THERE is often a progress in human affairs which may indeed be retarded, but which nothing can arrest. Moving on with slow and silent steps, it is marked only by comparing distant periods. The causes which produce it are either so minute as to be invisible, or, if preceived, are too numerous and complicated to be subject to human controul. Of such sort is the advancement of knowledge among the negroes of this country. It is so striking, as to be obvious to a man of the most ordinary observation. Every year adds to the number of those who can read and write; and he who has made any proficiency in letters, becomes a little centre of instruction to others. This increase of knowledge is the principal agent in evolving the spirit we have to fear. The love of freedom, sir, is an inborn sentiment, which the God of nature has planted deep in the heart: long may it be kept under by the arbitrary institutions of society; but, at the first favourable moment, it springs forth, and flourishes with a vigour that defies all check. This celestial spark, which fires the breast of the savage, which glows in that of the philosopher, is not extinguished in the bosom of the slave. It may be buried in the embers; but it still lives; and the breath of knowledge kindles it into flame. Thus we find, sir, there never have been slaves in any country, who have not seized the first favorable opportunity to revolt.

IN our infant country, where population and wealth increase with unexampled rapidity, the progress of liberal knowledge is proportionally great. In this vast march of the mind, the blacks, who are far behind us, may be supposed to advance at a pace equal to our own; but, sir, the fact is, they are likely to advance much faster. The growth and multiplication of our towns tend a thousand ways to enlighten and inform them. The very nature of our government, which leads us to recur perpetually to the discussion of natural rights, favors speculation and enquiry. By way of marking the prodigious change which a few years has made among this class of men, compare the late conspiracy with the revolt under lord Dunmore. In the one case, a few solitary individuals flocked to that standard, under which they are sure to find protection. In the other, they, in a body, of their own accord, combine a plan for asserting their claims, and rest their safety on success alone. The difference is, that then they fought freedom merely as a good; now they also claim it as a right. This comparison speaks better than volumes the change I insist upon.

... THERE is one argument to which I have not even hinted; but which some may think of more weight than any other;—I mean the ease whith which they may become the tools of a foreign enemy.

Granting that the danger from themselves is slight or remote, this, it must be confessed, depends upon an event that is altogether un-certain. War is sometimes inevitable; no human prudence can guard against an event that may be brought about by the insolence, the injustice, or the caprice of *any* nation. Whenever we are involved in this calamity, if our enemies hold out the lure of freedom, they will have, in every negro, a decided friend. The passage is easy from friends to auxiliaries: little address would be necessary to excite in-surrection; to put arms into their hands, and to convert a willing multitude into a compact and disciplined army. Those who did not openly join him would be secretly his friends and spies. In such a situation, as no vigilance could guard us against surprise, so neither would any line of conduct secure us from danger. Precaution would provoke resistance, and neglect would invite it. In short, sir, they may be considered as a piece of artillery, huge and seemingly un-manageable, but which the most unskilful of our enemies may play off against us.

IF, then our danger is continually increasing, and the only tem-porising policy, which has been contemplated, is more likely to ac-celerate than retard its progress; let us turn our attention to those remedies which propose a perfect cure of the mighty evil. This grand desideratum can be effected only by emancipation, or transportation. I will take a short view of their respective merits and practicability.

THE most zealous advocates for a general emancipation, seeing the impossibility of amalgamating such discordant materials, confess the necessity of qualifying the gift of freedom, by denying the negroes some of the most important privileges of a citizen. Considering them, then, in this subordinate station, the friends of the scheme say, or may say, that men, when admitted to the rights of individual liberty and property, have patiently borne the deprivation of civil rights: That the negroes, with us, would be in that mean state which is most propitious to peace and order; not enough in want of the goods of life, to be turbulent from despair; nor possessing them in such abun-dance as to be factious from ambition. They may cite the peasantry of Europe as a signal instance of this tolerant disposition; since *there*, a small part of the community keeps the other from a participation of civil rights, though nature has made not an atom of difference between the two orders; whilst, *here*, she has set a visible and immutable boundary, which is thought to separate an inferior from a superior class. That, excluded from the ownership of lands, and the more honorable occupations of life, they would necessarily continue to be what they now are, tradesmen, labourers, and household servants. That inasmuch as the man who labours for himself, will do more work, and do it better, than he who labours for another, the State would gain by the change, though individuals might seem to lose. That those who, by superior industry, or frugality, became rich, would form an intermediate class, which would be a fence against the possible enterprises of the rest: and the better to effect a difference of interests, that the more wealthy and reputable should be allowed certain political rights; which indulgence would prove, not only a considerable prop to the State, but also a powerful incitement to honest industry. In one word, it is said that their privileges and restraints would equally conduce to insure the public tranquility; since the advantages we conceded would make them contented; while those we with-held would make us secure.

THIS project, it must be confessed, has an air of plausibility, which seduces at first sight. But, on cool examination, I am compelled to pronounce it one of those closet schemes, which do more honor to the heart than to the head. Apt as we are to estimate by comparison, and to prize more highly the little we want, than the much we possess, it may be fairly inferred, that the negroes, if once emancipated, would never rest satisfied with any thing short of perfect equality. The taste would but whet their appetite. This growing discontent, joined to our conduct towards them, still more contemptuous than unjust, would generate a secret animosity, which a foreign enemy would easily convert into an open breach. May they not even become the auxiliaries of domestic faction; or the fit engine of any artful and enterprising leader? In short, this scheme seems to me to be the offspring of an ingenious philanthropy, rather than of true political wisdom. Let us, then, turn our attention to the plan of transportation.

THE number of Blacks and Mulattoes, in Virginia, must now exceed three hundred thousand. Their annual increase is little short of fifteen thousand. The expence of transporting to Africa this number alone, at twenty pounds a head, would be a million of dollars; so that, at a glance, we see that this plan of removal is beyond the resources of the State. To the West-Indies, if their inhabitants were willing to admit so dangerous a body; if the government of the United States would consent to the cruel exile; if the enlightened legislature, of which you are now a member, could sanctify so derogatory a purpose, the sympathy and humanity of individual slaveholders would never suffer them to be torn from those tender attachments which now soften the miseries of servitude, to suffer still greater in a foreign land. It then remains to be seen, if they can be colonized in some part of the American continent. This, I confess, is my last remaining hope. I know the expence attending its execution; the prejudices of our fellow citizens; and the length of time necessary to carry it into beneficial operation. But it must be remembered, that we have only a choice of evils; and it is the part of wisdom to select the least. The following hints I submit to your serious and candid consideration.

THAT application be made to the United States, to procure from the Spanish government, or to furnish from its own territory, such a tract of country as shall be deemed sufficient for the colony proposed. The consideration of future peace would recommend the western side of the Mississippi. Present convenience and oeconomy would advise a purchase of some part of the Indian country, comprehended within the limits of the state of Georgia.

THAT this colony be under the protection and immediate government of this state, or the United States, until it contained a number of inhabitants sufficient to manage their own concerns: and that it be exclusively appropriated to the colonization and residence of people of colour.

THAT a poll tax be laid on every negro and mulatto, to be collected by officers appointed in each county, who should vest the money so raised, in the purchase of slaves to be sent at the expence of the state, to the colony. By this arrangement the tax would be more oeconomically and advantageously managed; and the diminution of slaves would be proportioned to the number, in every part of the state.

THAT there be an additional and a heavier tax on all females above the age of puberty; and a bounty on the exportation of every female of any age. To increase the effect, the bounty may be reduced by one half, after the age of twenty-five, or thirty. This part of the plan (which I owe to an ingenious friend) will have a double effect in inducing many to export their female slaves: and when a girl under fourteen or fifteen is sent out of the country, six or eight unborn negroes are probably sent with her. It may be thought unworthy of the laws to encourage this dishonorable traffic, but the most imperious of all laws, that of self-preservation, authorises it. And with us, the power of sending them out of the country is exercised with peculiar moderation and humanity.

THAT emancipation should be encouraged rather than checked: and the better to induce the voluntary migration of free negroes and mulattoes, every accommodation and indulgence should be shewn them in the colony. They should also be assisted in removing their persons and effects; and additional taxes and disabilities may be imposed on them here.

IF all these means united does not diminish the number faster than the natural increase, all those born in a year, at stated periods, every fifth or sixth, for example, may be emancipated at a certain age, on condition of their migrating, or paying a stipulated sum....

Documents for Chapter 3

Black Americans in a White Republic

1. Cæsar Sarter, "Essay on Slavery," Newburyport, Mass., *The Essex Journal and Merrimack Packet*, August 17, 1774

Cæsar Sarter had been a slave in Newburyport, Massachusetts, near Boston, before the American Revolution, but he had gained his freedom before the fighting broke out. He was one of those obscure individuals who suddenly emerged as a spokesman for Africans in America. More than simply attacking slavery, Sarter asked Americans to live by the golden rule and set the enslaved Africans free.

Please to give the following Address, *To those who are Advocates for holding the Africans in Slavery*, a place in your next, and you will oblige one, who is a well-wisher to his brethren, who are now in that unhappy state.

As this is a time of great anxiety and distress among you, on account of the infringement not only of your Charter rights; but of the *natural rights and privileges of freeborn men*; permit a poor, though *freeborn*, African, who, in his youth, was trapanned into Slavery and who has born the galling yoke of bondage for more than twenty years; though at last, by the blessing of God, has shaken it off, to tell you, and that from experience, that as *Slavery* is the greatest, and consequently most to be dreaded, of all temporal calamities: So its opposite, *Liberty*, is the greatest temporal good, with which you can be blest! The importance of which, you can clearly evince to the world you are sensible of, by your manly and resolute struggles to preserve it. Your fore fathers, as I have been often informed, left their native country, together with many dear friends, and came into this country, then a howling wilderness inhabited, only, by savages, rather choosing, under the protection of their GOD, to risk their lives, among those merciless wretches, than submit to tyranny at home: While, therefore, this conduct gives you their exalted sense of the worth of LIBERTY, at the same time, it shews their utmost abhorrence of that CURSE OF CURSES, *SLAVERY.*—Your Parliament, to their immortal honor be it mentioned, to whom *WE* feel that gratitude, which so high a favour naturally produces, in an ingenious mind have exerted their utmost abilities, to put a final stop, to so iniquitous a business, as the Slave Trade is: That they have not succeeded in their laudable endeavours was not their fault: But they were defeated by his late Excellency only—Now, if you are sensible, that slavery is in itself, and in it consequences, a great evil; why will you not pity and relieve the poor, distressed, enslaved Africans?— Who, though they are entitled to the same *natural rights of mankind* that you are, are, nevertheless, groaning in bondage! A bondage which will only terminate with life: To them a shocking consideration indeed! Though too little, I fear, thought of by most of you who enjoy the profits of their labour. As the importation of slaves into this Province, is generally laid aside, I shall not pretend a refutation of the arguments, generally brought in support of it; but request you, to let that excellent rule given by our Saviour, *to do to others, as you would, that they should do to you*, have its due weight with you. Though the thought be shocking—for a few minutes, suppose that you were trapanned away.—The husband from the dear wife of his bosom—the wife from her affectionate husband—children from their fond parents— or parents from their tender and beloved offspring, whom, not an hour before, perhaps, they were fondling in their arms, and in whom they were promising themselves much future happiness: Suppose, I say that you were thus ravished from such a blissful situation, and plunged into miserable slavery, in a distant quarter of the globe: Or suppose you were accompanied by your wife and children, parents and brethren, manacled by your side—harrowing thought! And that after having suffered the most amazing hardships, your fetters were knocked from your galled limbs, only to expose you to keener an-guish!—Exposed to sale, with as little respect to decency, as though you were a brute! And after all this, if you were unwilling to part with all you held dear, even without the privilege of droping a tear over your dear friends, who were clinging round you; equally dread-ing the cruel separation, which would probably prove an endless one, you must be plied with that conclusive argument, the cat-o'nine tails, to reduce you to what your inhuman masters would call Reason. Now, are you willing all this should befall you? If you can lay your hand on your breast, and solemnly affirm that you should; Why then go on and prosper! For your treatment of the Africans is an exact com-pliance with the abovementioned rule: But if, on the other hand, your conscience answers in the negative; Why, in the name of Heaven, will you suffer such a gross violation of that rule by which your conduct must be tried, in that day, in which you must be accountable for all your actions, to that impartial Judge, who hears the groans of the oppressed and who will, sooner or later, avenge them of their oppressors! I need not tell *you*, who are acquainted with the scriptures that this kind of oppression is discountenanced by them. Many pas-sages, to this purpose, might be adduced, but I shall at present, men-tion but one, Exod chap 20 ver. 16 *"And he that stealeth a man, and selleth him, or if he be found in his hand, he shall surely be put to death."*

Though we are brought from a land of ignorance, it is as certain, that we are brought from a land of comparative innocence—from a land that flows, as it were, with Milk and Honey—and the greater part of us carried, where we are, not only deprived of every comfort of life: But subjected to all the tortures that a most cruel inquisitor could invent, or a capricious tyrant execute, and where we are likely, from the vicious examples before us, to become tenfold more the children of satan, than we should, probably, have been in our native country. Though 'tis true, that some of our wars proceed from petty discords among ourselves, it is as true, that the greater part of them, and those the most bloody, are occasioned, in consequence of the Slave trade.—Though many think we are happier here, than there, and will not allow us the privilege of judging for ourselves, they are certainly in an error. Every man is the *best* judge of his *own* happiness, and every heart *best* knows its *own* bitterness.—While I feel the loss of my country, and my friends, I can, by sad experience, adopt that expression in *Prov.* 25th Chap. 20 verse. *As he that taketh away a garment in cold weather, and as vinegar upon nitre, so is he that singeth songs to a heavy heart.* Let me, who have now no less than eleven relatives suffering in bondage beseech you good people, to attend to the request of a poor African, and consider the evil consequences, and gross heinousness of reducing to, and retaining in slavery a free people. Would you desire the preservation of your own liberty? As the first step let the oppressed Africans be liberated; then, and not till then, may you with confidence and consistency of conduct, look to Heaven for a blessing on your endeavours to knock the shackles with which your task masters are hampering you, from your own feet. On the other hand, if you are still determined to harden your hearts, and turn a deaf ear to our complaints, and the calls of God, in your present Calamities; Only be pleased to recollect the miserable end of Pharoah, in Consequence of his refusal to set those at Liberty, whom he had unjustly reduced to cruel servitude. Remember the fate of Miriam for despising an Ethiopean woman, *Numb.* 12 chap. 1st and 10th. verses. I need not point out the absurdity of your exertions for liberty, while you have slaves in your houses, for one minute's reflection is, methinks, sufficient for that purpose.—You who are deterred from liberating your slaves, by the consideration of the ill consequences to yourselves must remember, that we were not the *cause* of our being brought here. If the compelling us, against our wills, to come here was a sin; to retain us, without our consent, now we are here, is, I think, equally culpable let ever so great inconvenience arising therefrom, accrue to you. Not to trespass too much on your patience; would you unite in this generous, this noble purpose of granting us liberty; Your honorable assembly, on our humble petition, would, I doubt not, free you from the trouble of us by making us grants in some back part of the country. If in this attempt to serve my countrymen, I have advanced any thing to the purpose, I pray it may not be the less noticed for coming from an African.

CÆSAR SARTER.

Newbury Port, August 12th, 1774.

2. Petitions of New England Slaves for Freedom (1773–1779)

The American Revolution mobilized slaves as well as free whites in the cause of freedom and equality as the rhetoric of natural rights spread from white revolutionaries to black bondspeople. The three petitions printed here, from slaves in Boston, Massachusetts, in 1773, and from Stratford and Fairfield, Connecticut, in 1779, were typical of many others that African slaves presented to state legislatures during the American war for independence. The Boston petition, which calls attention to the Spanish system of *coratacion*, whereby slaves were entitled to work for money to buy their freedom and were entitled to it after accumulating their market value, demonstrates that even in faraway New England slaves had a keen sense of how the institution of slavery operated in other, distant parts of the Americas.

Province of the Massachusetts Bay To His Excellency Thomas Hutchinson, Esq; Governor; To the Honorable His Majesty's Council, and To the Honorable House of Representatives in General Court assembled at Boston, the 6th Day of *January*, 1773.

The humble PETITION of many Slaves, living in the Town of Boston, and other Towns in the Province is this, namely

That your Excellency and Honors, and the Honorable the Representatives would be pleased to take their unhappy State and Condition under your wise and just Consideration.

We desire to bless God, who loves Mankind, who sent his Son to die for their Salvation, and who is no respecter of Persons; that he hath lately put it into the Hearts of Multitudes on both Sides of the Water, to bear our Burthens, some of whom are Men of great Note and Influence; who have pleaded our Cause with Arguments which we hope will have their weight with this Honorable Court.

We presume not to dictate to your Excellency and Honors, being willing to rest our Cause on your Humanity and Justice; yet would beg Leave to say a Word or two on the Subject.

Although some of the Negroes are vicious, (who doubtless may be punished and restrained by the same Laws which are in Force against other of the King's Subjects) there are many others of a quite different Character, and who, if made free, would soon be able as well as willing to bear a Part in the Public Charges; many of them of good natural Parts, are discreet, sober, honest, and industrious; and may it not be said of many, that they are virtuous and religious, although their Condition is in itself so unfriendly to Religion, and every moral Virtue except *Patience*. How many of that Number have there been, and now are in this Province, who have had every Day of their Lives imbittered with this most intollerable Reflection, That, let their Behaviour be what it will, neither they, nor their Children to all Generations, shall ever be able to do, or to possess and enjoy any Thing, no, not even *Life itself*, but in a Manner as the *Beasts that perish.*

We have no Property! We have no Wives! No Children! We have no City! No Country! But we have a Father in Heaven, and we are determined, as far as his Grace shall enable us, and as far as our degraded contemptuous Life will admit, to keep all his Commandments: Especially will we be obedient to our Masters, so long as God in his sovereign Providence shall *suffer* us to be holden in Bondage.

It would be impudent, if not presumptuous in us, to suggest to your Excellency and Honors any Law or Laws proper to be made, in relation to our unhappy State, which, although our greatest Unhappiness, is not our *Fault*; and this gives us great Encouragement to pray and hope for such Relief as is consistent with your Wisdom, Justice, and Goodness.

We think Ourselves very happy, that we may thus address the Great and General Court of this Province, which great and good Court is to us, the best Judge, under God, of what is wise, just and good.

We humbly beg Leave to add but this one Thing more: We pray for such Relief only, which by no Possibility can ever be productive of the least Wrong or Injury to our Masters; but to us will be as Life from the dead.

Signed,
FELIX

Boston, April 20th, 1773

Sir, The efforts made by the legislative of this province in their last sessions to free themselves from slavery, gave us, who are in that deplorable state, a high degree of satisfaction. We expect great things from men who have made such a noble stand against the designs of their *fellow-men* to enslave them. We cannot but wish and hope Sir, that you will have the same grand object, we mean civil and religious liberty, in view in your next session. The divine spirit of *freedom*, seems to fire every humane breast on this continent, except such as are bribed to assist in executing the execrable plan.

We are very sensible that it would be highly detrimental to our present masters, if we were allowed to demand all that of *right* belongs to us for past services; this we disclaim. Even the *Spaniards*, who have not those sublime ideas of freedom that English men have, are conscious that they have no right to all the services of their fellow-men, we mean the *Africans*, whom they have purchased with their money; therefore they allow them one day in a week to work for themselves, to enable them to earn money to purchase the residue of their time, which they have a right to demand in such portions as they are able to pay for (a due appraizement of their services being first made, which always stands at the purchase money.) We do not pretend to dictate to you Sir, or to the Honorable Assembly, of which you are a member. We acknowledge our obligations to you for what you have already done, but as the people of this province seem to be actuated by the principles of equity and justice, we cannot but expect your house will again take our deplorable case into serious consideration, and give us that ample relief which, *as men*, we have a natural right to.

But since the wise and righteous governor of the universe, has permitted our fellow men to make us slaves, we bow in submission to him, and determine to behave in such a manner as that we may have reason to expect the divine approbation of, and assistance in, our peaceable and lawful attempts to gain our freedom.

We are willing to submit to such regulations and laws, as may be made relative to us, until we leave the province, which we determine to do as soon as we can, from our joynt labours procure money to transport ourselves to some part of the Coast of *Africa*, where we propose a settlement. We are very desirous that you should have instructions relative to us, from your town, therefore we pray you to communicate this letter to them, and ask this favor for us.

In behalf of our fellow slaves in this province, and by order of their Committee.

Peter Bestes,
Sambo Freeman,
Felix Holbrook,
Chester Joie.

For the Representative of the town of Thompson.

To the Honbl. General Assembly of the State of Connecticut to be held at Hartford on the Second Thursday of Instant May [1779]— The Petition of the Negroes in the Towns of Stratford and Fairfield in the County of Fairfield who are held in a State of Slavery humbly sheweth—

That many of your Petitioners, were (as they verily believe) most unjustly torn, from the Bosom of their dear Parents, and Friends, and without any Crime, by them committed, doomed, and bound down, to perpetual Slavery; and as if the Perpetrators of this horrid Wickedness, were conscious (that we poor Ignorant Africans, upon the least Glimering Sight, derived from a Knowledge of the Sense and Practice of civilized Nations) should Convince them of their Sin, they have added another dreadful Evil, that of holding us in gross Ignorance, so as to render Our Subjection more easy and tolerable. may it please your Honours, we are most grievously affected, under the Consideration of the flagrant Injustice; Your Honours who are nobly contending, in the Cause of Liberty, whose Conduct excites the Admiration, and Reverence, of all the great Empires of the World; will not resent, our thus freely animadverting, on this detestable Practice; altho our Skins are different in Colour, from those whom we serve, Yet Reason & Revelation join to declare, that we are the Creatures of that God, who made of one Blood, and Kindred, all the Nations of the Earth; we perceive by our own Reflection, that we are endowed with the same Faculties with our masters, and there is nothing that leads us to a Belief, or Suspicion, that we are any more obliged to serve them, than they us, and the more we Consider of this matter, the more we are Convinced of our Right (by the Laws of Nature and by the whole Tenor of the Christian Religion, so far as we have been taught) to be free; we have endeavoured rightly to understand what is our Right, and what is our Duty, and can never be convinced that we were made to be Slaves. Altho God almighty may justly lay this, and more upon us, yet we deserve it not, from the hands of Men. we are impatient under the grievous Yoke, but our Reason teaches us that it is not best for us to use violent measures, to cast it off; we are also convinced, that we are unable to extricate ourselves from our abject State; but we think we may with the greatest Propriety look up to your Honours, (who are the fathers of the People) for Relief. And we not only groan under our own burden, but with concern, & Horror, look forward, & contemplate, the miserable Condition of our Children, who are training up, and kept in Preparation, for a like State of Bondage, and Servitude. we beg leave to submit, to your Honours serious Consideration, whether it is consistent with the present Claims, of the united States, to hold so many Thousands, of the Race of Adam, our Common Father, in perpetual Slavery. Can human Nature endure the Shocking Idea? can your Honours any longer Suffer this great Evil to prevail under your Government: we entreat your Honours, let no considerations of Publick Inconvenience deter your Honours from interposing in behalf of your Petitioners; we ask for nothing, but what we are fully persuaded is ours to Claim. we beseech your Honours to weigh this matter in the Scale of Justice, and in your great Wisdom and goodness, apply such Remedy as the Evil does require; and let your Petitioners rejoice with your Honours in the Participation with your Honours

of that inestimable Blessing, *Freedom* and your Humble Petitioners,
as in Duty bound shall ever pray &c.

dated in Fairfield the 11th Day of May A D 1779—

prime a Negro man
servant to Mr.
Vam A. Sturge
of Fairfield
his
Prince X a Negro man
mark
servant of Capt. Stephen Jenings
of Fairfield —
in Behalf of themselves and
the other Petitioners

3. A Letter from Benjamin Banneker to the Secretary of State (Philadelphia, 1792)

Benjamin Banneker, a free black from Maryland, was a talented mathematician, astronomer, and surveyor who stood as living refutation of the theory of black inferiority. One of the three men who surveyed the site for the new federal capital in Washington, he wrote this letter to Thomas Jefferson in 1791 while sending the Secretary of State a copy of his manuscript for a soon-to-be-published *Almanac*. In writing Jefferson, Banneker was subtly chiding the Secretary for his earlier comments on black inferiority, published in Jefferson's widely read *Notes on the State of Virginia* (1784). The Georgetown *Weekly Ledger* had already reported the arrival of Banneker as part of the surveying team and called him "an Ethiopian whose abilities as surveyor and astronomer already prove that Mr. Jefferson's concluding that that race of men were void of mental endowment was without foundation."

On August 30, 1791, Jefferson responded to Banneker, thanking him for the almanac, which indicated "that nature has given to our black brethren talents equal to those of the other colors of men." Only their "degraded condition" suppressed the development of Africans. Jefferson said that he had forwarded Banneker's almanac to the Academy of Science in Paris as proof against the doctrine of black inferiority.

Maryland, Baltimore County, August 19, 1791.

SIR,

I am fully sensible of the greatness of that freedom, which I take with you on the present occasion; a liberty which seemed to me scarcely allowable, when I reflected on that distinguished and dignified station in which you stand, and the almost general prejudice and prepossession, which is so prevalent in the world against those of my complexion.

I suppose it is a truth too well attested to you, to need a proof here, that we are a race of beings, who have long labored under the abuse and censure of the world; that we have long been looked upon with an eye of contempt; and that we have long been considered rather as brutish than human, and scarcely capable of mental endowments.

Sir, I hope I may safely admit, in consequence of that report which hath reached me, that you are a man far less inflexible in sentiments of this nature, than many others; that you are measurably friendly, and well disposed towards us; and that you are willing and ready to lend your aid and assistance to our relief, from those many distresses, and numerous calamities, to which we are reduced.

Now Sir, if this is founded in truth, I apprehend you will embrace every opportunity, to eradicate that train of absurd and false ideas and opinions, which so generally prevails with respect to us; and that your sentiments are concurrent with mine, which are, that one universal Father hath given being to us all; and that he hath not only made us all of one flesh, but that he hath also, without partiality, afforded us all the same sensations and endowed us all with the same faculties; and that however variable we may be in society or religion, however diversified in situation or color, we are all of the same family, and stand in the same relation to him.

Sir, if these are sentiments of which you are fully persuaded, I hope you cannot but acknowledge, that it is the indispensible duty of those, who maintain for themselves the rights of human nature, and who possess the obligations of Christianity, to extend their power and influence to the relief of every part of the human race, from whatever burden or oppression they may unjustly labor under; and this, I apprehend, a full conviction of the truth and obligation of these principles should lead all to.

Sir, I have long been convinced, that if your love for yourselves, and for those inestimable laws, which preserved to you the rights of human nature, was founded on sincerity, you could not but be solicitous, that every individual, of whatever rank or distinction, might with you equally enjoy the blessings thereof; neither could you rest satisfied short of the most active effusion of your exertions, in order to their promotion from any state of degradation, to which the un-justifiable cruelty and barbarism of men may have reduced them.

Sir, I freely and cheerfully acknowledge, that I am of the African race, and in that color which is natural to them of the deepest dye; and it is under a sense of the most profound gratitude to the Supreme Ruler of the Universe, that I now confess to you, that I am not under that state of tyrannical thraldom, and inhuman captivity, to which too many of my brethren are doomed, but that I have abundantly tasted of the fruition of those blessings, which proceed from that free and unequalled liberty with which you are favored; and which, I hope, you will willingly allow you have mercifully received, from the immediate hand of that Being, from whom proceedeth every good and perfect Gift.

Sir, suffer me to recal to your mind that time, in which the arms and tyranny of the British crown were exerted, with every powerful effort, in order to reduce you to a state of servitude: look back, I entreat you, on the variety of dangers to which you were exposed; reflect on that time, in which every human aid appeared unavailable, and in which even hope and fortitude wore the aspect of inability to the conflict, and you cannot but be led to a serious and grateful sense of your miraculous and providential preservation; you cannot but acknowledge, that the present freedom and tranquility which you enjoy you have mercifully received, and that it is the peculiar blessing of Heaven.

This, Sir, was a time when you clearly saw into the injustice of a state of slavery, and in which you had just apprehensions of the horrors of its condition. It was now that your abhorrence thereof was so excited, that you publicly held forth this true and invaluable doctrine, which is worthy to be recorded and remembered in all succeeding ages: "We hold these truths to be self-evident, that all men are created equal; that they are endowed by their Creator with certain unalienable rights, and that among these are, life, liberty, and the pursuit of happiness."

Here was a time, in which your tender feelings for yourselves had engaged you thus to declare, you were then impressed with proper ideas of the great violation of liberty, and the free possession of those blessings, to which you were entitled by nature; but, Sir, how pitiable is it to reflect, that although you were so fully convinced of the benevolence of the Father of Mankind, and of his equal and impartial distribution of these rights and privileges, which he hath conferred upon them, that you should at the same time counteract his mercies, in detaining by fraud and violence so numerous a part of my brethren, under groaning captivity and cruel oppression, that you should at the same time be found guilty of that most criminal act, which you professedly detested in others, with respect to yourselves.

I suppose that your knowledge of the situation of my brethren, is too extensive to need a recital here; neither shall I presume to prescribe methods by which they may be relieved, otherwise than by recommending to you and all others, to wean yourselves from those narrow prejudices which you have imbibed with respect to them, and as Job proposed to his friends, "put your soul in their souls' stead;" thus shall your hearts be enlarged with kindness and benevolence towards them; and thus shall you need neither the direction of myself or others, in what manner to proceed herein.

And now, Sir, although my sympathy and affection for my brethren hath caused my enlargement thus far, I ardently hope, that your candor and generosity will plead with you in my behalf, when I make known to you, that it was not originally my design; but having taken up my pen in order to direct to you, as a present, a copy of an Almanac, which I have calculated for the succeeding year, I was unexpectedly and unavoidably led thereto.

This calculation is the production of my arduous study, in this my advanced stage of life; for having long had unbounded desires to become acquainted with the secrets of nature, I have had to gratify my curiosity herein, through my own assiduous application to Astronomical Study, in which I need not recount to you the many difficulties and disadvantages, which I have had to encounter.

And although I had almost declined to make my calculation for the ensuing year, in consequence of that time which I had allotted therefor, being taken up at the Federal Territory, by the request of Mr. Andrew Ellicott, yet finding myself under several engagements to Printers of this state, to whom I had communicated my design, on my return to my place of residence, I industriously applied myself thereto, which I hope I have accomplished with correctness and accuracy; a copy of which I have taken the liberty to direct to you, and which I humbly request you will favorably receive; and although you may have the opportunity of perusing it after its publication, yet I choose to send it to you in manuscript previous thereto, that thereby you might not only have an earlier inspection, but that you might also view it in my own hand writing. . . .

4. Absalom Jones and Richard Allen, *A Narrative of the Proceedings of the Black People, During the Late Awful Calamity in Philadelphia, in the year 1793* (Philadelphia, 1794)

Both Absalom Jones and Richard Allen gained their freedom during the American Revolution after many years in slavery. They became the most important leaders of the new nation's largest free black community, located in Philadelphia and swelled after the war by private manumissions and also by the arrival of runaway slaves from the South. Both founded free black churches—the first in the North—and both became tireless advocates of abolitionism. They took special care in their pamphlet, excerpted here, to show that black Philadelphians acted honorably during the ghastly yellow fever epidemic of 1793 in Philadelphia. While whites fled the city in droves, Jones and Allen mobilized black members of the community to nurse the sick, drive the death carts, and bury the dead. While defending the behavior of free blacks against charges by Mathew Carey, one of Philadelphia's printers, that they had charged exorbitantly for their services, they reminded the city (where the federal government was located) of the continuing problem of slavery.

An Address to those who keep Slaves, and approve the practice.

The judicious part of mankind will think it unreasonable, that a superior good conduct is looked for, from our race, by those who stigmatize us as men, whose baseness is incurable, and may therefore be held in a state of servitude, that a merciful man would not doom a beast to; yet you try what you can to prevent our rising from the state of barbarism, you represent us to be in, but we can tell you, from a degree of experience, that a black man, although reduced to the most abject state human nature is capable of, short of real madness, can think, reflect, and feel injuries, although it may not be with the same degree of keen resentment and revenge, that you who have been and are our great oppressors, would manifest if reduced to the pitiable condition of a slave. We believe if you would try the experiment of taking a few black children, and cultivate their minds with the same care, and let them have the same prospect in view, as to living in the world, as you would wish for your own children, you would find upon the trial, they were not inferior in mental endowments.

We do not wish to make you angry, but excite your attention to consider, how hateful slavery is in the sight of that God, who hath destroyed kings and princes, for their oppression of the poor slaves; Pharaoh and his princes with the posterity of king Saul, were destroyed by the protector and avenger of slaves. Would you not suppose the Israelites to be utterly unfit for freedom, and that it was impossible for them to attain to any degree of excellence? Their history shews how slavery had debased their spirits. Men must be wilfully blind and extremely partial, that cannot see the contrary effects of liberty and slavery upon the mind of man; we freely confess the vile habits often acquired in a state of servitude, are not easily thrown off; the example of the Israelites shews, who with all that Moses could do to reclaim them from it, still continued in their former habits more or less; and why will you look for better from us? Why will you look for grapes from thorns, or figs from thistles? It is in our posterity enjoying the same privileges with your own, that you ought to look for better things.

When you are pleaded with, do not you reply as Pharaoh did, "wherefore do ye Moses and Aaron, let the people from their work, behold the people of the land, now are many, and you make them rest from their burdens." We wish you to consider, that God himself was the first pleader of the cause of slaves.

That God who knows the hearts of all men, and the propensity of a slave to hate his oppressor, hath strictly forbidden it to his chosen people, "thou shalt not abhor an Egyptian, because thou wast a stranger in his land. Deut. xxiii. 7." The meek and humble Jesus, the great pattern of humanity, and every other virtue that can adorn and dignify men, hath commanded to love our enemies, to do good to them that hate and despitefully use us. We feel the obligations, we wish to impress them on the minds of our black brethren, and that we may all forgive you, as we wish to be forgiven; we think it a great mercy to have all anger and bitterness removed from our minds; we appeal to your own feelings, if it is not very disquieting to feel yourselves under the dominion of a wrathful disposition.

If you love your children, if you love your country, if you love the God of love, clear your hands from slaves, burden not your children or country with them. Our hearts have been sorrowful for the late bloodshed of the oppressors, as well as the oppressed, both appear guilty of each others blood, in the sight of him who said, he that sheddeth man's blood, by man shall his blood be shed.

Will you, because you have reduced us to the unhappy condition our colour is in, plead our incapacity for freedom, and our contented condition under oppression, as a sufficient cause for keeping us under the grievous yoke? We have shewn the cause of our incapacity, we will also shew, why we appear contented; were we to attempt to plead with our masters, it would be deemed insolence, for which cause they appear as contented as they can in your sight, but the dreadful insurrections they have made, when opportunity has offered, is enough to convince a reasonable man, that great uneasiness and not contentment, is the inhabitant of their hearts.

God himself hath pleaded their cause, he hath from time to time raised up instruments for that purpose, sometimes mean and contemptible in your sight; at other times he hath used such as it hath pleased him, with whom you have not thought it beneath your dignity to contend, many have been convinced of their error, condemned their former conduct, and become zealous advocates for the cause of those, whom you will not suffer to plead for themselves.

5. Petition of North Carolina Blacks to Congress, January 23, 1797

Absalom Jones, pastor of the St. Thomas's African Episcopal Church of Philadelphia, was the probable drafter of this affecting petition. The petitioners were four North Carolina blacks who had been freed by their masters but then pursued by whites who wished to reenslave them under a law passed in 1788 that allowed for the capture of manumitted slaves still in the state. After a debate, Congress refused to accept the petition from what southern members regarded as fugitive slaves—a sign of the waning of the abolitionist impulse. This is the earliest extant petition to Congress from black Americans.

To the President, Senate, and House of Representatives. [*]

The Petition and Representation of the under-named Freemen, respectfully showeth:—

That, being of African descent, late inhabitants and natives of North Carolina, to you only, under God, can we apply with any hope of effect, for redress of our grievances, having been compelled to leave the State wherein we had a right of residence, as freemen liberated under the hand and seal of humane and conscientious masters, the validity of which act of justice in restoring us to our native right of freedom, was confirmed by judgment of the Superior Court of North Carolina, wherein it was brought to trial; yet, not long after this decision, a law of that State was enacted, under which men of cruel disposition, and void of just principle, received countenance and authority in violently seizing, imprisoning, and selling into slavery, such as had been so emancipated; whereby we were reduced to the necessity of separating from some of our nearest and most tender connexions, and of seeking refuge in such parts of the Union where more regard is paid to the public declaration in favor of liberty and

Annals of Congress, 4th Cong., 2nd Sess. (Washington, D. C., 1855), 2015–18.

the common right of man, several hundreds, under our circumstances, having, in consequence of the said law, been hunted day and night, like beasts of the forest, by armed men with dogs, and made a prey of as free and lawful plunder. Among others thus exposed, I, Jupiter Nicholson, of Perquimans county, North Carolina, after being set free by my master, Thomas Nicholson, and having been about two years employed as a seaman in the service of Zachary Nickson, on coming on shore, was pursued by men with dogs and arms; but was favored to escape by night to Virginia, with my wife, who was manumitted by Gabriel Cosan, where I resided about four years in the town of Portsmouth, chiefly employed in sawing boards and scantling; from thence I removed with my wife to Philadelphia, where I have been employed, at times, by water, working along shore, or sawing wood. I left behind me a father and mother, who were manumitted by Thomas Nicholson and Zachary Dickson; they have been since taken up, with a beloved brother, and sold into cruel bondage.

I, Jacob Nicholson, also of North Carolina, being set free by my master, Joseph Nicholson, but continuing to live with him till, being pursued day and night, I was obliged to leave my abode, sleep in the woods, and stacks in the fields, &c., to escape the hands of violent men who, induced by the profit afforded them by law, followed this course as a business; at length, by night, I made my escape, leaving a mother, one child, and two brothers, to see whom I dare not return.

I, Job Albert, manumitted by Benjamin Albertson, who was my careful guardian to protect me from being afterwards taken and sold, providing me with a house to accommodate me and my wife, who was liberated by William Robertson; but we were night and day hunted by men armed with guns, swords, and pistols, accompanied with mastiff dogs; from whose violence, being one night apprehensive of immediate danger, I left my dwelling, locked and barred, and fastened with a chain, being at some distance from it, while my wife was by my kind master locked up under his roof. I heard them break into my house, where, not finding their prey, they got but a small booty, a handkerchief of about a dollar value, and some provisions; but, not long after, I was discovered and seized by Alexander Stafford, William Stafford, and Thomas Creesy, who were armed with guns and clubs. After binding me with my hands behind me, and a rope round my arms and body, they took me about four miles to Hartford prison, where I lay four weeks, suffering much for want of provision; from thence, with the assistance of a fellow-prisoner, (a white man,) I made my escape, and for three dollars was conveyed, with my wife, by a humane person, in a covered wagon by night, to Virginia, where, in the neighborhood of Portsmouth, I continued unmolested about four years, being chiefly engaged in sawing boards and plank. On being advised to move Northward, I came with my wife to Phila-delphia, where I have labored for a livelihood upwards of two years, in Summer mostly along shore in vessels and stores, and sawing wood in the Winter. My mother was set free by Phineas Nickson, my sister by John Trueblood, and both taken up and sold into slavery, myself deprived of the consolation of seeing them, without being exposed to the like grievous oppression.

I, Thomas Pritchet, was set free by my master Thomas Pritchet, who furnished me with land to raise provisions for my use, where I built myself a house, cleared a sufficient spot of woodland to produce ten bushels of corn; the second year about fifteen, and the third, had as much planted as I suppose would have produced thirty bushels; this I was obliged to leave about one month before it was fit for gathering, being threatened by Holland Lockwood, who married my said master's widow, that if I would not come and serve him, he would apprehend me, and send me to the West Indies; Enoch Ralph also threatening to send me to jail, and sell me for the good of the country: being thus in jeopardy, I left my little farm, with my small stock and utensils, and my corn standing, and escaped by night into Virginia, where shipping myself for Boston, I was, through stress of weather landed in New York, where I served as a waiter for seventeen months; but my mind being distressed on account of the situation of my wife and children, I returned to Norfolk in Virginia, with a hope of at least seeing them, if I could not obtain their freedom; but finding I was advertised in the newspaper, twenty dollars the reward for apprehending me, my dangerous situation obliged me to leave Virginia, disappointed of seeing my wife and children, coming to Philadelphia, where I resided in the employment of a waiter up-ward of two years.

In addition to the hardship of our own case, as above set forth, we believe ourselves warranted, on the present occasion, in offering to your consideration the singular case of a fellow-black now confined in the jail of this city, under sanction of the act of General Government, called the Fugitive Law, as it appears to us a flagrant proof how far human beings, merely on account of color and complexion, are, through prevailing prejudice, outlawed and excluded from common justice and common humanity, by the operation of such partial laws in support of habits and customs cruelly oppressive. This man, having been many years past manumitted by his master in North Carolina, was under the authority of the aforementioned law of that State, sold again into slavery, and, after having served his purchaser upwards of six years, made his escape to Philadelphia, where he has resided eleven years, having a wife and four children; and, by an agent of the Carolina claimer, has been lately apprehended and committed to prison, his said claimer, soon after the man's escaping from him, having advertised him, offering a reward of ten silver dollars to any person that would bring him back, or five times that sum to any person that would make due proof of his being killed, and no questions asked by whom.

We beseech your impartial attention to our hard condition, not only with respect to our personal sufferings, as freemen, but as a class of that people who, distinguished by color, are therefore with a degrading partiality, considered by many, even of those in eminent stations, as unentitled to that public justice and protection which is the great object of Government. We indulge not a hope, or presume to ask for the interposition of your honorable body, beyond the extent of your Constitutional power or influence, yet are willing to believe your serious, disinterested, and candid consideration of the premises, under the benign impressions of equity and mercy, producing upright exertion of what is in your power, may not be without some salutary effect, both for our relief as a people, and towards the removal of obstructions to public order and well-being.

If, notwithstanding all that has been publicly avowed as essential principles respecting the extent of human right to freedom; notwithstanding we have had that right restored to us, so far as was in the power of those by whom we were held as slaves, we cannot claim the privilege of representation in your councils, yet we trust we may address you as fellow-men, who, under God, the sovereign Ruler of the Universe, are intrusted with the distribution of justice, for the terror of evil-doers, the encouragement and protection of the innocent, not doubting that you are men of liberal minds, susceptible of benevolent feelings and clear conception of rectitude to a catholic extent, who can admit that black people (servile as their condition generally is throughout this Continent) have natural affections, social and domestic attachments and sensibilities; and that, therefore, we may hope for a share in your sympathetic attention while we represent that the unconstitutional bondage in which multitudes of our fellows in complexion are held, is to us a subject sorrowfully affecting; for we cannot conceive their condition (more especially those who have been emancipated and tasted the sweets of liberty, and again reduced to slavery by kidnappers and man-stealers) to be less afflicting or deplorable than the situation of citizens of the United States, captured and enslaved through the unrighteous policy prevalent in Algiers. We are far from considering all those who retain slaves as wilful oppressors, being well assured that numbers in the State from whence we are exiles, hold their slaves in bondage, not of choice, but possessing them by inheritance, feel their minds burdened under the slavish restraint of legal impediments to doing that justice which they are convinced is due to fellow-rationals. May we not be allowed to consider this stretch of power, morally and politically, a Governmental defect, if not a direct violation of the declared fundamental principles of the Constitution; and finally, is not some remedy for an evil of such magnitude highly worthy of the deep inquiry and unfeigned zeal of the supreme Legislative body of a free and enlightened people? Submitting our cause to God, and humbly craving your best aid and influence, as you may be favored and directed by that wisdom which is from above, wherewith that you may be eminently dignified and rendered conspicuously, in the view of nations, a blessing to the people you represent, is the sincere prayer of your petitioners.

> JACOB NICHOLSON,
> JUPITER NICHOLSON, his mark,
> JOB ALBERT, his mark,
> THOMAS PRITCHET, his mark.

PHILADELPHIA, *January* 23, 1797.

6. James Forten, *Letters from a Man of Colour on a Late Bill Before the Senate of Pennsylvania* (Philadelphia, 1813)

James Forten, born into one of colonial Philadelphia's rare free black families, fought as a powderboy on a privateer during the American Revolution. After the war, he took up his father's occupation of sailmaking and became the city's most successful black businessman. As the abolitionist spirit waned in the early nineteenth century and white racial hostility hemmed in northern free blacks, Forten put aside his natural reticence and became a forceful spokesman for black rights. In the pamphlet excerpted here, he argued against the enactment of special measures to stop the flow of black migrants into Pennsylvania or to fasten special disabilities on them. Such measures began to receive consideration in Pennsylvania as early as 1805, but because of efforts such as Forten's they never passed. Forten's reminders to white Pennsylvanians of their own revolutionary heritage demonstrates his keen knowledge of history and his ability to invoke the elevated principles of the Revolution to defend the rights of black Americans.

LETTER I.

WE hold this truth to be self-evident, that GOD created all men equal, and is one of the most prominent features in the Declaration of Independence, and in that glorious fabrick of collected wisdom, our noble Constitution. This idea embraces the Indian and the European, the Savage and the Saint, the Peruvian and the Laplander, the white Man and the African, and whatever measures are adopted subversive of this inestimable privilege, are in direct violation of the letter and spirit of our Constitution, and become subject to the animadversion of all, particularly those who are deeply interested in the measure.

These thoughts were suggested by the promulgation of a late bill, before the Senate of Pennsylvania, to prevent the emigration of people of colour into this state. It was not passed into a law at this session and must in consequence lay over until the next, before when we sincerely hope, the white men, whom we should look upon as our protectors, will have become convinced of the inhumanity and impolicy of such a measure, and forbear to deprive us of those inestimable treasures, Liberty and Independence. This is almost the only state in the Union wherein the African race have justly boasted of rational liberty and the protection of the laws, and shall it now be said they have been deprived of that liberty, and publickly exposed for sale to the highest bidder? Shall colonial inhumanity that has marked many of us with shameful stripes, become the practice of the people of Pennsylvania, while Mercy stands weeping at the miserable spectacle? People of Pennsylvania, descendants of the immortal Penn, doom us not to the unhappy fate of thousands of our countrymen in the Southern States and the West Indies; despise the traffick in blood, and the blessing of the African will for ever be around you. Many of us are men of property, for the security of which, we have hitherto looked to the laws of our blessed state, but should this become a law, our property is jeopardized, since the same power which can expose to sale an unfortunate fellow creature, can wrest from him those estates, which years of honest industry have accumulated. Where shall the poor African look for protection, should the people of Pennsylvania consent to oppress him? We grant there are a number of worthless men belonging to our colour, but there are laws of sufficient rigour for their punishment, if properly and duly enforced. We wish not to screen the guilty from punishment, but with the guilty do not permit the innocent to suffer. If there are worthless men, there are also men of merit among the African race, who are useful members of Society. The truth of this let their benevolent institutions and the numbers clothed and fed by them witness. Punish the guilty man of colour to the utmost limit of the laws, but sell him not to slavery! If he is in danger of becoming a publick charge prevent him! If he is too indolent to labour for his own subsistence, compel him to do so; but sell him not to slavery. By selling him you do not make him better, but commit a wrong, without benefitting the object of it or society at large. Many of our ancestors were brought here more than one hundred years ago; many of our fathers, many of ourselves, have fought and bled for the Independence of our country. Do not then expose us to sale. Let not the spirit of the father behold the son robbed of that Liberty which he died to establish, but let the motto of our Legislators be: "The Law knows no distinction.". . .

LETTER II.

Those patriotick citizens, who, after resting from the toils of an arduous war, which achieved our Independence and laid the foundation of the only reasonable Republick upon earth, associated together, and for the protection of those inestimable rights for the establishment of which they had exhausted their blood and treasure, framed the Constitution of Pennsylvania, have by the ninth article, declared, that "All men are born equally free and independent, and have certain inherent and indefeasible rights, among which are those of enjoying life and liberty." Under the restraint of wise and well administered laws, we cordially unite in the above glorious sentiment, but by the bill upon which we have been remarking, it appears as if the committee who drew it up mistook the sentiment expressed in this article, and do not consider us as men, or that those enlightened statesmen who formed the constitution upon the basis of experience, intended to exclude us from its blessings and protection. If the former, why are we not to be considered as men. Has the GOD who made the white man and the black, left any record declaring us a different species. Are we not sustained by the same power, supported by the same food, hurt by the same wounds, wounded by the same wrongs, pleased with the same delights, and propagated by the same means. And should we not then enjoy the same liberty, and be protected by the same laws.—We wish not to legislate, for our means of information and the acquisition of knowledge are, in the nature of things, so circumscribed, that we must consider ourselves incompetent to the task; but let us, in legislation, be considered as men. It cannot be that the authors of our Constitution intended to exclude us from its benefits, for just emerging from unjust and cruel mancipation, their souls were too much affected with their own deprivations to commence the reign of terror over others. They knew we were deeper skinned than they were, but they acknowledged us as men, and found that many an honest heart beat beneath a dusky bosom. They felt that they had no more authority to enslave us, than England had to tyrannize over them. They were convinced that if amenable to the same laws in our actions, we should be protected by the same laws in our rights and privileges. Actuated by these sentiments they adopted the glorious fabrick of our liberties, and declaring "all men" free, they did not particularize white and black, because they never supposed it would be made a question whether *we were men or not.* Sacred be the ashes, and deathless be the memory of those heroes who are dead; and revered be the persons and the characters of those who still exist and lift the thunders of admonition against the traffick in blood. And here my brethren in colour, let the tear of gratitude and the sigh of regret break forth for that great and good man, who lately fell a victim to the promiscuous fury of death, in whom you have lost a zealous friend, a powerful, an herculean advocate; a sincere adviser, and one who spent many an hour of his life to break your fetters, and ameliorate your condition—I mean the ever to be lamented Dr. BENJAMIN RUSH. . . .

Let us put a case, in which the law in question operates peculiarly hard and unjust.—I have a brother, perhaps, who resides in a distant part of the Union, and after a separation of years, actuated by the same fraternal affection which beats in the bosom of a white man, he comes to visit me. Unless that brother be registered in twenty four hours after, and be able to produce a certificate to that effect, he is liable, according to the second and third sections of the bill, to a fine of twenty dollars, to arrest, imprisonment and sale. Let the unprejudiced mind ponder upon this, and then pronounce it the justifiable act of a free people, if he can. To this we trust our cause, without fear of the issue. The unprejudiced must pronounce any act tending to deprive a free man of his right, freedom and immunities, as not only cruel in the extreme, but decidedly unconstitutional both as regards the letter and spirit of that glorious instrument. The same power which protects the white man, should protect A MAN OF COLOUR.

LETTER III.

The evils arising from the bill before our Legislature, so fatal to the rights of freemen, and so characteristick of European despotism, are so numerous, that to consider them all, would extend these numbers further than time or my talent will permit me to carry them. The concluding paragraph of my last number, states a case of peculiar hardship, arising from the second section of this bill, upon which I cannot refrain from making a few more remarks. The man of color receiving as a visiter any other person of colour, is bound to turn informer, and rudely report to the Register, that a friend and brother has come to visit him for a few days, whose name he must take within twenty four hours, or forfeit a sum which the iron hand of the law is authorized to rend from him, partly for the benefit of the REGISTER. Who is this Register? A man, and exercising an office, where ten dollars is the fee for each delinquent, will probably be a cruel man and find delinquents where they really do not exist. The poor black is left to the merciless gripe of an avaricious REGISTER, without an appeal, in the event, from his tyranny or oppression! O miserable race, born to the same hopes, created with the same feeling, and destined for the same goal, you are reduced by your fellow creatures below the brute. The dog is protected and pampered at the board of his master, while the poor African and his descendant, whether a Saint or a felon, is branded with infamy, registered as a slave, and we may expect shortly to find a law to prevent their increase, by taxing them according to numbers, and authorizing the Constables to seize and confine every one who dare to walk the streets without a collar on his neck!—What have the people of colour been guilty of, that they more than others, should be compelled to register their houses, lands, servants and *Children*. Yes, ye rulers of the black man's destiny, reflect upon this: our *Children* must be registered, and bear about them a certificate, or be subject to imprisonment and fine. You, who are perusing this effusion of feeling, are you a parent? Have you children around whom your affections are bound, by those delightful bonds which none but a parent can know? Are they the delight of your prosperity, and the solace of your afflictions? If all this be true, to you we submit our cause. The parent's feeling cannot err. By your verdict will we stand or fall—by your verdict, live slaves or freemen. It is said, that the bill does not extend to children, but the words of the bill are, "Whether as an *inmate, visiter, hireling, or tenant, in his or her house or room*." Whether this does not embrace every soul that can be in a house, the reader is left to judge; and whether the father should be bound to register his child, even within the twenty four hours after it is brought into the world, let the father's feelings determine. This is the fact, and our children sent on our lawful business, not having sense enough to understand the meaning of such proceedings, must show their certificate of registry or be borne to prison. The bill specifies neither age nor sex—designates neither the honest man or the vagabond—but like the fretted porcupine, his quills aim its deadly shafts promiscuously at all.

For the honour and dignity of our native state, we wish not to see this bill pass into a law, as well as for its degrading tendency towards us; for although oppressed by those to whom we look for protection, our grievances are light compared with the load of reproach that must be heaped upon our commonwealth. The story will fly from the north to the south, and the advocates of slavery, the traders in human blood, will smile contemptuously at the once boasted moderation and humanity of Pennsylvania! What, that place, whose institutions for the prevention of Slavery, are the admiration of surrounding states and of Europe, become the advocate of mancipation and wrong, and the oppressor of the free and innocent!—Tell it not in Gath! publish it not in the streets of Askelon! lest the daughters of the Philistines rejoice! lest the children of the uncircumcised triumph!

It is to be hoped that in our Legislature there is patriotism, humanity, and mercy sufficient, to crush this attempt upon the civil liberty of freemen, and to prove that the enlightened body who have hitherto guarded their fellow creatures, without regard to the colour of the skin, will still stretch forth the wings of protection to that race, whose persons have been the scorn, and whose calamities have been the jest of the world for ages. We trust the time is at hand when this obnoxious Bill will receive its death warrant, and freedom still remain to cheer the bosom of A MAN OF COLOUR.

Letter IV.

I proceed again to the consideration of the bill of *unalienable* rights belonging to black men, the passage of which will only tend to show, that the advocates of emancipation can enact laws more degrading to the free man, and more injurious to his feelings, than all the tyranny of slavery, or the shackles of infatuated despotism. And let me here remark, that this unfortunate race of humanity, although protected by our laws, are already subject to the fury and caprice of a certain set of men, who regard neither humanity, law nor privilege. They are already considered as a different species, and little above the brute creation. They are thought to be objects fit for nothing else than lordly men to vent the effervescence of their spleen upon, and to tyrannize over, like the bearded Musselman over his horde of slaves. Nay, the Musselman thinks more of his horse, than the generality of people do of the despised black!—Are not men of colour sufficiently degraded? Why then increase their degradation. It is a well known fact, that black people, upon certain days of publick jubilee, dare not be seen after twelve o'clock in the day, upon the field to enjoy the times; for no sooner do the fumes of that potent devil, Liquor, mount into the brain, than the poor black is assailed like the destroying Hyena or the avaricious Wolf! I allude particularly to the FOURTH OF JULY!—Is it not wonderful, that the day set apart for the festival of Liberty, should be abused by the advocates of Freedom, in endeavouring to sully what they profess to adore. If men, though they know that the law protects all, will dare, in defiance of law, to execute their hatred upon the defenceless black, will they not by the passage of this bill, believe him still more a mark for their venom and spleen.—Will they not believe him completely deserted by authority, and subject to every outrage brutality can inflict—too surely they will, and the poor wretch will turn his eyes around to look in vain for protection. Pause, ye rulers of a free people, before you give us over to despair and violation—we implore you, for the sake of humanity, to snatch us from the pinnacle of ruin, from that gulph, which will swallow our rights, as fellow creatures; our privileges, as citizens; and our liberties, as men!

There are men among us of reputation and property, as good citizens as any men can be, and who, for their property, pay as heavy taxes as any citizens are compelled to pay. All taxes, except personal, fall upon them, and still even they are not exempted from this degrading bill. The villanous part of the community, of all colours, we wish to see punished and retrieved as much as any people can. Enact laws to punish them severely, but do not let them operate against the innocent as well as the guilty. Can there be any generosity in this? Can there be any semblance of justice, or of that enlightened conduct which is ever the boasted pole star of freedom? By no means. This bill is nothing but the ignus fatuus of mistaken policy! . . .

LETTER V.

. . . By the third section of this bill, which is its peculiar hardship, the police officers are authorized to apprehend any black, whether a vagrant or a man of reputable character, who cannot produce a Certificate that he has been registered. He is to be arrayed before a justice, who is thereupon to commit him to prison!—The jailor is to advertise a Freeman, and at the expiration of six months, if no owner appear for this degraded black, he is to be *exposed to sale*, and if not sold to be confined at hard labour for seven years!!—Man of feeling, read this!—No matter who, no matter where. The Constable, whose antipathy generally against the black is very great, will take every opportunity of hurting his feelings!—Perhaps, he sees him at a distance, and having a mind to raise the boys in hue and cry against him, exclaims, "Halloa! Stop the Negro!" The boys, delighting in the sport, immediately begin to hunt him, and immediately from a hundred tongues, is heard the cry—*"Hoa, Negro, where is your Certificate!"*—Can any thing be conceived more degrading to humanity!—Can any thing be done more shocking to the principles of Civil Liberty! A person arriving from another state, ignorant of the existence of such a law, may fall a victim to its cruel oppression. But he is to be advertised, and if no owner appear—How can an owner appear for a man who is free and belongs to no one!—If no owner appear, he is exposed for sale!—Oh, inhuman spectacle: found in no unjust act, convicted of no crime, he is barbarously sold, like the produce of the soil, to the highest bidder, or what is still worse, for no crimes, without the inestimable privilege of a trial by his peers, doomed to the dreary walls of a prison for the term of seven tedious years!—My God, what a situation is his. Search the legends of tyranny and find no precedent. No example can be found in all the reigns of violence and oppression, which have marked the lapse of time. It stands alone. It has been left for Pennsylvania, to raise her ponderous arm against the liberties of the black, whose greatest boast has been, that he resided in a State where Civil Liberty, and sacred Justice were administered alike to all.—What must be his reflections now, that the asylum he had left from mancipation has been destroyed, and that he is left to suffer, like Daniel of old, with no one but his God to help him! Where is the bosom that does not heave a sigh for his fall, unless it be callous to every sentiment of humanity and mercy?

The fifth section of this bill, is also peculiarly hard, inasmuch as it prevents freemen from living where they please.—Pennsylvania has always been a refuge from slavery, and to this state the Southern black, when freed, has flown for safety. Why does he this! When masters in many of the Southern states, which they frequently do, free a particular black, unless the Black leaves the state in so many hours, any person resident of the said state, can have him arrested and again sold to Slavery:—The hunted black is obliged to flee, or remain and be again a Slave. I have known persons of this description sold three times after being first emancipated. Where shall he go? Shut every state against him, and, like Pharoah's kine, drive him into the sea.—Is there no spot on earth that will protect him! Against their inclination, his ancestors were forced from their homes by traders in human flesh, and even under such circumstances, the wretched offspring are denied the protection you afford to brutes.

It is in vain that we are forming societies of different kinds to ameliorate the condition of our unfortunate brethren, to correct their morals and to render them not only honest but useful members to society. All our efforts, by this bill, are despised, and we are doomed to feel the lash of oppression:—As well may we be outlawed, as well may the glorious privileges of the Gospel, be denied us, and all endeavours used to cut us off from happiness hereafter as well as here!—The case is similar, and I am much deceived if this bill does not destroy the morals it is intended to produce.

I have done. My feelings are acute, and I have ventured to express them without intending either accusation or insult to any one. An appeal to the heart is my intention, and if I have failed, it is my great misfortune, not to have had a power of eloquence sufficient to convince. But I trust the eloquence of nature will succeed, and that the law-givers of this happy Commonwealth will yet remain the Blacks' friend, and the advocates of Freemen, is the sincere wish of A MAN OF COLOUR.

7. George Lawrence, *An Oration on the Abolition of the Slave Trade* (New York, 1813)

Beginning on January 1, 1808, when the slave trade was abolished by Congress, African-Americans began to celebrate January 1 as their fourth of July. Black leaders in the cities of the North ordinarily gave sermons of thanks on this day, and many of them were published. In these sermons, they often compared their deliverance to that of the Jews, but they also reminded their parishioners—and the nation at large—that slavery was far from dead and, in fact, was growing rapidly in the South. More and more, they became the conscience for a nation that was sacrificing its founding ideals to the economic interests of those who profited from slave labor.

... My brethren, the land in which we live gives us the opportunity rapidly to advance the prosperity of liberty. This government founded on the principles of liberty and equality, and declaring them to be the free gift of God, if not ignorant of their declaration, must enforce it; I am confident she wills it, and strong forbodings of it is discernable. The nothern sections of the union is fast conceding, and the southern must comply, although so biased by interest, that they have become callous to the voice of reason and justice; yet as the continual droppings of water has a tendency to wear away the hardest and most flinty substance, so like wise shall we, abounding in good works, and causing our examples to shine forth as the sun at noon day, melt their callous hearts, and render sinewless the arm of sore oppression. My brethren, you who are enroled and proudly march under the banners of the Mutual Relief, and Wilberforce Societies, consider your important standings as incorporated bodies, and walk worthy of the name you bear, cling closely to the paths of virtue and morality, cherish the plants of peace and temperance; by doing this you shall not only shine as the first stars in the firmament, and do honor to your worthy patrons, but immortalize your names. Be zealous and vigilent, be always on the alert to promote the welfare of your injured brethren; then shall providence shower down her blessings upon your heads, and crown your labors with success. It has been said by your enemies, that your minds were not calculated to receive a sufficient store of knowledge, to fit you for beneficial or social societies; but your incorporation drowned that assertion in contempt; and now let shame cover their heads, and blushes crimson their countenances. In vain they fostered a hope that our unfavorable circumstances would bear them out in their profane insinuations. But is that hope yet alive? No; or do we know where to find it? If it is to be found, it must be in the dark abysses of ignorance and folly, too little, too trifling for our notice.

There could be many reasons given, to prove that the mind of an African is not inferior to that of an European; yet to do so would be superfluous. It would be like adding hardness to the diamond, or lustre to the sun. There was a time whilst shrouded in ignorance, the African was estimated no higher than beasts of burthen, and while their minds were condensed within the narrow compass of slavery, and all their genius damped by the merciless power of cruel masters, they moved in no higher sphere. Their nature was cramped in infancy, and depraved in riper years, vice was showed them for virtue, and for their labor and industry, the scourge was their only reward. Then did they seem dead to a better state, but it was because they were subject to arbitrary power; and then did their proud oppressors assert, though against their better judgment, that they were destined by nature to no better inheritance. But their most prominent arguments are lighter than vanity, for vacuous must the reasons of that man have been, who dared to assert that genius is confined to complexion, or that nature knows difference in the immortal soul of man: No! the noble mind of a Newton could find room, and to spare, within the tenement of many an injured African.

My brethren, the time is fast approaching when the iron hand of oppression must cease to tyranize over injured innocence, and very different are the days that we see, from those that our ancestors did; yet I know that there are thousands of our enemies who had rather see us exterminated from off the earth, than partake of the blessings that they enjoy; but their malice shall not be gratified; they will, though it blast their eyes, still see us in prosperity. Our day star is arisen, and shall perform its diurnal revolutions, until nature heself shall change; and my heart glows with the idea, and kindles with joy, as my eye catches its radient beams dispersing the dark clouds of ignorance and superstition. The spring is come, and the autumn nigh at hand, when the rich fruits of liberty shall be strewed in the paths of every African, or descendant, and the olive hedge of peace encompass them in from their enemies. . . .

And, O! thou father of the universe and disposer of events, thou that called from a dark and formless mass this fair system of nature, and created thy sons and daughters to bask in the golden streams and rivulets contained therein; this day we have convened under thy divine auspices, its not to celebrate a political festivity, or the at-chievement of arms by which the blood of thousands were spilt, contaminating thy pure fields with human gore! but to commemorate a period brought to light by thy wise counsel, who stayed the hand of merciless power, and with hearts expanded with gratitude for thy providences, inundated in the sea of thy mercies we further crave thy fostering care. O! wilt thou crush that power that still holds thousands of our brethren in bondage, and let the sea of thy wisdom wash its very dust from off the face of the earth; let LIBERTY unfurl her banners, FREEDOM and JUSTICE reign triumphant in the world, universally.

READING FURTHER

THE BACKGROUND FOR UNDERSTANDING the American revolutionists' confrontation with slavery is richly developed in David Brion Davis, *The Problem of Slavery in Western Culture* (Ithaca, N. Y., 1966). In the sequel, *The Problem of Slavery in the Age of Revolution, 1770–1823* (Ithaca, N. Y., 1975), Davis treats the trans-Atlantic antislavery movement during and after the American Revolution. Those interested in a synthesis of these important studies and Davis's most recent thoughts on the subject can turn to his *Slavery and Human Progress* (New York, 1987). Edmund S. Morgan also provides a provocative general statement on the paradox of slavery in a society founded on the principles of republicanism in *American Slavery, American Freedom: The Ordeal of Colonial Virginia* (New York, 1975). Jean R. Soderlund, in *Quakers & Slavery: A Divided Spirit* (Princeton, N. J., 1985), shows the struggles of a vanguard antislavery religious group to extricate itself from "the peculiar institution," and George S. Brookes takes the reader inside the world of America's voice of conscience in his biography of Anthony Benezet—*Friend Anthony Benezet* (Philadelphia, 1937). Winthrop D. Jordan also portrays the rise of revolutionary consciousness on the problem of slavery, and provides an extended treatment of prior thinking about race among the colonists, in *White Over Black: American Attitudes Toward the Negro, 1550–1812* (Chapel Hill, N. C., 1968).

More specific studies about the attempts of Americans to dismantle the system of slave labor—and the limitations of these efforts—are Duncan J. MacLeod, *Slavery, Race and the American Revolution* (Cambridge, Mass., 1974); Arthur Zilversmit, *The First Emancipation: The Abolition of Slavery in the North* (Chicago, 1967); Robert McColley, *Slavery and Jeffersonian Virginia* (Urbana, Ill., 1964); and Gary B. Nash and Jean R. Soderlund, *Freedom by Degrees: Emancipation and Its Aftermath in Pennsylvania* (New York, 1990). All of these can take on new meaning after reading about how earlier historians treated the question of slavery in the era of revolution. Especially important for this are the essays by Staughton Lynd, "On Turner, Beard, and Slavery," in Lynd, *Class Conflict, Slavery, and the United States Constitution* (Indianapolis, Ind., 1967); Fawn M. Brodie, "Who Defends the Abolitionists?" in Martin B. Duberman, ed., *The Antislavery Vanguard: New Essays on the Abolitionists* (Princeton, N. J., 1965); and Duberman, "The Northern Response to Slavery," in *ibid*.

Two important essays for understanding the compromises over slavery made at the Constitutional Convention of 1787 are Staughton Lynd, "The Compromise of 1787," in his *Class Conflict, Slavery, and the United States Constitution*; and Paul Finkelman, "Slavery and the Constitutional Convention: Making a Covenant with Death," in Richard Beeman, Stephen Botein, and Edward C. Carter II, *Beyond Confederation: Origins of the Constitution and American National Identity* (Chapel Hill, N. C., 1987). The further concessions made to slaveholders by the first Congress that met under the newly ratified Constitution is the subject of Howard A. Ohline's essay, "Slavery, Economics, and Congressional Politics, 1790," *Journal of Southern History*, 46

(1980). The eclipse of the antislavery impulse is followed in Donald L. Robinson, *Slavery in the Structure of American Politics, 1765–1820* (New York, 1971). The road from antislavery to proslavery ideology in the early nineteenth century can be traced in Larry E. Tise, *Proslavery: A History of the Defense of Slavery in America, 1701–1840* (Athens, Ga., 1987).

Studies of black Americans in the revolutionary and postrevolutionary eras have only occasionally commanded the attention of historians until recent years. Two pioneering books that look at the role of African-Americans in the Revolution and what happened to former slaves in the North after the conflict are Benjamin Quarles, *The Negro in the American Revolution* (Chapel Hill, N. C., 1961), and Leon Litwack, *North of Slavery: The Negro in the Free States, 1790–1860* (Chicago, 1961). More recent studies about postrevolutionary African-American life and consciousness include Floyd J. Miller, *The Search for a Black Nationality: Black Colonization and Emigration, 1787–1863* (Urbana, Ill., 1975); Leonard P. Curry, *The Free Black in Urban America, 1800–1850: The Shadow of a Dream* (Chicago, 1981); and Gary B. Nash, *Forging Freedom: The Formation of Philadelphia's Black Community, 1720–1840* (Cambridge, Mass., 1988).

Several biographies provide attractive ways of understanding the postrevolutionary world as African-Americans experienced it. Charles H. Wesley's biographies of two important Boston and Philadelphia black leaders are *Richard Allen: Apostle of Freedom* (Washington, D. C., 1935); and *Prince Hall: Life and Legacy* (Philadelphia, 1977). Another important study of Richard Allen is Carol V. R. George, *Segregated Sabbaths: Richard Allen and the Rise of Independent Black Churches, 1760–1845* (New York, 1973). Charles Akers' *Phyllis Wheatley* (Boston, 1985) is a poignant study, as is Lamont D. Thomas, *Rise to Be a People: A Biography of Paul Cuffe* (Urbana, Ill., 1986). A group portrait of Philadelphia's black leaders is provided by Julie Winch in *Philadelphia's Black Elite: Activism, Accommodation, and the Struggle for Autonomy, 1787–1840* (Philadelphia, 1988).

The importance of the independent black churches to community life in the postwar period makes several recent studies of Afro-Christianity especially valuable. Fascinating accounts can be found in the early chapters of Gayraud S. Wilmore's *Black Religion and Black Radicalism: An Interpretation of the Religious History of Afro-American People* (New York, 1973) and Vincent Harding's *There is a River: The Black Struggle for Freedom in America* (New York, 1981). Also valuable is Albert J. Raboteau, "Richard Allen and the African Church Movement," in Leon Litwack and August Meier, eds., *Black Leaders in the Nineteenth Century* (Urbana, Ill., 1989); and Will B. Gravely, "The Rise of African Churches in America (1786–1822): Re-examining the Contexts," *Journal of Religious Thought*, 41 (1984).

INDEX